social savvy

a teenager's guide to feeling confident in any situation

JUDITH RÉ with
MEG F. SCHNEIDER

A FIRESIDE BOOK
Published by Simon and Schuster

NEW YORK   LONDON   TORONTO
SYDNEY   TOKYO   SINGAPORE

Fireside
Simon & Schuster Building
Rockefeller Center
1230 Avenue of the Americas
New York, NY 10020

First Fireside Edition 1992

FIRESIDE and colophon are registered trademarks of Simon & Schuster Inc.

Designed by Bonni Leon
Manufactured in the United States of America

10 9 8 7 6 5 4 3

Library of Congress Cataloging-in-Publication Data is available

ISBN 0-671-69023-X
ISBN 0-671-74198-5 (pbk)

The illustrations in this book were created by Marco A. Hernandez.
SOCIAL SAVVY is a registered service mark of Judith Ré.

contents

To my parents, Frank and Adelia: with love and laughter, you showed me the true meaning of Social Savvy

And to my wonderful husband, John Morgan, whose constant encouragement was the wind beneath my wings

And to my sister, Elena, for always knowing which side the fork went on!

J.R.

———

To Linda Goldman,
Whose Savvy Glows

M.S.

acknowledgments

I would like to thank the following people for all of their encouragement: Sigi Brauer, who said yes to the Academie, and Patricia Cutler, whose creativity is endless; Jan Hurley Clare, Kathleen White, Donna Leaman, Candy Beagles, Margaret Neil, Elena Valdez, Kristen Knight: thanks for all the weekends; Thom Egan for believing in the program; Meg Schneider, a first-rate collaborator with no equal; my agent, Carol Mann, for taking me on board and Carole Lalli for giving me a second chance; Gary Shechtman for his sound legal advice; also C. Whitney Ward, Vivian Deuschel, and Lilli Leaf for their support of the Academie. Thanks to Louie Gignac for telling Albert to try. A special thanks to the staffs of the Ritz-Carlton hotels in Boston and Washington, D.C., the Four Seasons hotel in Seattle, and the Stouffers hotel in Cleveland. Finally, my heartfelt thanks and admiration to Laura Yorke, one of the finest editors around and a cut above others: thanks for always being there to listen, to encourage, to answer every question; thanks for being a true professional and a very dear person.

J.R.

how savvy are you? an introduction

Have you ever found yourself talking to someone whose name you can't remember even though you've just been introduced?
Have you ever cut your carrots at a très élégant restaurant only to have them torpedo off your plate and land on someone else's lap?
Have you ever been a guest at a good friend's house and accidentally broken his parents' precious crystal vase?

In short, have you ever found yourself involved in a social situation that has left you feeling terribly confused, truly upset, or unbelievably embarrassed?

Of course you have! After all, you're alive. You are a thinking, feeling human being and certain circumstances are bound to bring up difficult emotions. None of us can ever feel perfectly relaxed in difficult-to-handle circumstances, which will always crop up. But, and this is a big but, there is a lot you can do to make yourself, and as a consequence those around you, more comfortable in these situations.

And that's what this book, *Social Savvy*, is all about. It will sharpen your social skills and give you a generous dose of practical know-how. It will exercise your common sense, develop your sensitivity, and strengthen your confidence. In short, it will make you feel more comfortable in your shoes. Social savvy is a quality of interacting with the world with ease and style. It allows you to trust in your ability to enter any social situation, be it a conversation with a long-lost relative, a fancy dinner party, a dance at school, or a luncheon at the French embassy. Social savvy is about taking control of circumstances instead of allowing them to frighten, intimidate, confuse, or embarrass you.

social savvy or good manners?

I hesitate to say that good manners are something this book will explore. But I hesitate only because of what I know the phrase "good manners" conjures up: little old ladies playing bridge, politely asking one another to pass the pot of tea, or your mother admonishing you to "watch your manners" as you noisily slurp the minestrone.

But that's the only reason I hesitate to compare good manners with social savvy. Social savvy, in fact, has a lot to do with good manners —except that it's the aspect of good manners you probably never think about. And for good reason. People usually forget to tell you the purpose of good manners, which I will get to later. (Perhaps it's because they've forgotten it themselves!) More often they just insist that you have them. And so, understandably, remembering good manners can feel like an unnatural burden that has nothing to do with real life.

But manners are anything but a burden. They are, in fact, your ticket to acquiring that thing called social savvy. Which brings me to the most basic reason for having good manners.

Good manners are not simply about doing what old Aunt Roberta would do, because that's the right way, or blindly following rules. Good manners are about being considerate, and feeling good when your thoughtfulness helps. They are about having respect for others whether they are younger, older, or just your age, and enjoying their respect in turn. They are about being sensitive to your surroundings and thanking not only your host but the elevator operator as well, and being appreciated for it. Good manners are not just for special occasions. They are for every moment and, most importantly, they are for you.

Social savvy is like a magical invisible cloak you can wear anywhere. You can't see it, but you can feel its protective warmth allowing you to comfortably step out into the world. Some people would call that cloak "good manners." I prefer "social savvy" because it seems fuller to me. Wiser. More far-reaching and helpful. Still, during those awkward moments when I have received a gift I dislike, or tried to cut my chicken only to see it streak across my plate onto the table, or found myself at a party with nothing to say, I have quietly thanked my lucky stars for my good manners.

On weekends I conduct a two-day program for young people on social savvy. My goal is to help them become more comfortable with the day-to-day social demands of their lives as well as the most exquisitely fine details of social etiquette. "After all," as I frequently proclaim, "you never know when you might be asked to greet the Spanish ambassador, dine with the President of the United States, or plan the invitations to a black-tie affair for 250 guests!" Embraced by the inviting and elegant surroundings of many lovely hotels across the country, we proceed through the potential land mines of making small talk, eating unusual delicacies, writing thank-you notes, dealing with restaurant bills, planning parties, and infinitely more.

---

class quote

Early in the weekend one fellow raised his hand and said, "Excuse me, Miss Judith. But I don't live in the Ritz. What's all this got to do with me?" I laughed and replied, "I know. I don't live here, either. But chewing on a hamburger with your mouth wide open at home looks just as awful as chewing on a slice of filet mignon with your mouth wide open at the Ritz. Don't forget. It's the same set of table manners . . . just different surroundings! And everyone knows we only have one mouth."

At first, I confess, I am occasionally greeted by a certain amount of doubt and even nervousness. I can just hear the unspoken thoughts as my charges dutifully settle in to hear my opening remarks: "I hope she doesn't expect too much!" "When will I need this?" "I just want to have fun!" "Doesn't she realize I don't live in the Ritz?" And worst of all, "What if I can't do it?"

But then something begins to happen. Very quickly it dawns on the participants in my program that there isn't a day that goes by in which something of my suggestions, observations, and instruction can't help.

Lunch in the school cafeteria, meeting a new classmate, resolving an argument with a good friend, competing on the softball team, and even something as uneventful as choosing a gift for someone you hardly know are all opportunities for exercising a little social savvy—and taking the sting away from that feeling of "Uh-oh. Did I do the right thing?"

So what had begun for some as an obligation to study good manners, and a fear of not being good enough, became a weekend in learning how to simply put their best foot forward and gain the confidence to handle almost any situation—be it on a camping trip, during a tennis tournament, while studying with friends for a test, or yes, while out to dinner at the Ritz.

It makes no difference how you label that quality of moving about the world with ease and style—"good manners" or "social savvy." What matters is how you do it and the positive results it can bring into your life.

getting along better with everyone

One of the most enduring benefits of social savvy, aside from the ability to handle an assortment of tricky situations, is the way it can draw people to you. Of course, not everyone will like you. Then again, you won't like everyone, either. But the consideration and sensitivity you will begin to extend to others will almost always have a profound effect on how these people treat you. Do remember, however, that the reason for giving is not to receive. "One good turn deserves another" is just a phrase. Real life doesn't work in such an exact fashion.

It is important to realize that no friend can give in the exact same way as you and no two sets of parents will have the same attitudes about important issues. Some friends are better at listening than others. Some parents are more relaxed about curfews than others. This is because everyone has their different strengths, weaknesses, and ideas. What matters is the whole picture—that your friends and family treat you as kindly and considerately as you treat them. With social savvy at your fingertips you will have the ability to bring out the best in the people most important to you and thus, quite frankly, get what you most want: their respect and affection.

My mother once said, while I was complaining about the way I had just been treated by a friend, "You can't control what other people do. You can only try to control what *you* do." It's important to remember that you are not responsible for everything that happens in a given situation. You can only do your best to be your best. If a close friend accuses you of "having the biggest mouth ever," even though you only let one small tidbit slip, you cannot wish his or her reaction away. If you accidentally write a thank-you note to the right person for the wrong gift and you receive an annoyed phone call instead of a good-humored one, you cannot control that, either. And if the waiter argues he gave you the proper change when you know he didn't, his opinion will exist for as long as he cares to keep it.

Your job, and the point of this book, is to help yourself feel more comfortable, no matter what the circumstances. If you build on your social strengths and strengthen your weaknesses, you'll enjoy your life a lot more.

how savvy are you?

Undoubtedly, you move about your world with plenty of social savvy. You have good friends, adults seem to like you, and days go by without your even once worrying, "Should I say this?" or "I wish I hadn't done that!" Still, there are those times when everything you know seems not to be enough. Sometimes fleeting, sometimes painfully long, these difficult moments can fill you with frustration and discomfort. They may even start to feel bigger than you and so much more powerful—which is exactly where we all go wrong. A situation should never be allowed to control you! You need to control it.

What do I mean?

Imagine you are trying to get off the phone gracefully with an extremely talkative friend. The conversation is dragging on endlessly.

Every time you are about to say, "I've really got to go now," your friend proclaims, "Oh, I forgot! Listen to this!" Would it surprise you to know there are ways to promptly, politely, and tactfully sign off? Trouble is, if you don't know how, you'll either fall asleep on the phone or hang up rudely and certainly upset your friend. In either case you'll be letting the situation control you. That just about always spells disaster.

So here is a brief inventory to help you uncover where a little extra social savvy could be of special help to you. Answer *yes* or *no* to each statement. You may discover that you, like most everyone else, have a lot of social savvy in some situations, and not so much in others.

the social savvy inventory

I would know what to do if . . .

friendship savvy

- I opened a gift in front of a friend, only to find I already owned the exact same thing.
- I overheard one good friend saying something very unfair about another good friend.
- Two of my best friends were arguing and each person wanted me to take his or her side.
- My friend repeatedly went out and bought the same clothes I had just purchased, happily announcing each time, "See! We're twins!"
- Someone phoned me and I wasn't at all in the mood to chat.

party savvy

- My mother wouldn't allow me to attend a party and I was afraid and embarrassed to tell my friends.
- I gave a party and I noticed my friends from camp weren't mixing with my friends from school.
- Someone I didn't invite to my party wanted to know why.
- I went to a party and realized I wasn't wearing the right thing.
- I walked into a party and realized I hardly knew anyone.
- I mistakenly called someone I had just met by the wrong name.
- I had to write a thank-you note for a gift I hated.

• I spilled a glass of water on the dinner table at a friend's house.
• While my new friend was outside, his or her mother walked into the room and said, "Oh. I don't believe I know you."
• I went to a friend's house to spend the weekend, but one hour after arriving, I realized I wanted to go home.
• I got into an argument with a friend who was visiting me and I decided I wanted him or her to go home.

dining savvy

• During a terrific spaghetti dinner at a restaurant, I looked down at my new shirt and realized I was splattered with sauce.
• I felt a huge sneeze coming on at the dinner table.
• I noticed I was the only one with crumbs and stains around my dinner plate.
• My dinner was served at a fancy restaurant, only I couldn't figure out which fork to use, or what the extra plates were for.
• I squeezed a lemon over my fish, but the juice landed squarely in my neighbor's eye.
• My guest at the dinner table was being left out of the family dinner conversation.

money savvy

• A waiter took one look at the tip I left and said, "That's all?"
• A group of friends wanted to go to a restaurant that I could not possibly afford.
• My friends asked me why my house was so small.
• Someone, after seeing the fancy house I lived in, asked if my father was rich.
• I spent all of my allowance and still had half a week to go.

savvy for difficult times

• I walked into a friend's house and his or her parents were shouting at each other very angrily.
• The mother of a good friend was very sick and I had to go up to her bedroom and say hello.

• My friend came for a visit, told me his or her parents were getting divorced, and then started to cry.

• A Jewish friend was going home for a Seder, and I wanted to wish him or her a nice time without sounding ignorant about what a Seder is.

• I accompanied a Catholic friend to his or her church to hear Christmas carols and then suddenly everyone knelt down to pray.

• A new girl in a wheelchair came to school and my friends would not stop staring.

What did you discover? Chances are you discovered that a number of the above commonplace circumstances would leave you thinking, "Uh-oh. What do I do now?" Well, you've come to the right book. The above list is only a small portion of the situations you will learn to handle with great ease. Getting stuck in a difficult situation or simply finding yourself in a circumstance you are not used to can be unsettling, and sometimes even painful. You can't hope to avoid these moments. They will often happen without warning, when you least expect them. That's life. But there is a lot you can do to prepare yourself so that you will be able to manage the moment and give everyone involved a chance to ease through the trouble spot with a minimum of bad feelings. As I said before, it's never completely up to you. You alone can't always make a trying moment a breeze. But if you don't at least do your part, that trying moment doesn't stand a chance of blowing over.

Social savvy is something everyone deserves. It will need a little time to develop inside you, but once it's there, it will never desert you. It is my hope that this book will serve as your guide to feeling as good as you can, anywhere and at any time, no matter what the circumstances. In the end, it's not so much what has happened, as it is what you choose to do about it.

1

putting

your

social

savvy

to work

ONE

the building blocks of social savvy

*N*ow that you know what I mean by social savvy, perhaps you're thinking it's time to go out there and give it a try. I say absolutely! It's never too soon to improve the way you relate to others. But don't expect miracles. Social savvy is not something that happens overnight. It's something that grows within you, molded by your own special personality and influenced by the experiences life brings your way. So don't be discouraged if you blunder through yet one more awkward moment at a party or find yourself saying the totally wrong thing to a needy friend.

Because social savvy is a little more complicated than it looks, I think it's a smart move to take a look at what I feel are the five basic building blocks. These are *responsibility, compromise, sensitivity, respect,* and *know-how.*

Take your time with the five questionnaires that appear in this chapter to find out how each of these building blocks could be more important to you, and how they might be applied to every aspect of your life, whether you're ringside at the circus, making a new friend, or dining at the Ritz. Each time you answer yes on a questionnaire, take note. It's an important clue to what you need to work on. Then consider the situations that follow in each "action" section. Some may be identical to things that have happened to you; some may not. That doesn't matter. What counts is understanding how the five building blocks described here can translate into action.

"What I do is my choice, and I will accept the consequences."

Do you talk on the phone all night, worried sick about the homework you still haven't touched?

Have you ever canceled a baby-sitting job at the last minute because a friend invited you to a dynamite party?

Have you ever finished cleaning out the garage only to hear your father call out, "It's only half done!"

Do you ever pretend to agree with your friends even when you don't, because you don't want to lose them?

Have you ever failed to do your part of a group school project because "things kept coming up"?

Do you visit your grandparents every time you say you will?

No matter what your friends tell you to do and no matter what everyone else around you is doing, what you do has to be your decision. After all, it will always be you who suffers with, or happily enjoys, the consequences. If you do something against your better judgment because a friend thinks you should, the unhappy results will be felt by you—not him or her. But if you stand on your own two feet and make the decisions that feel right for you, then you will feel good about yourself. The same goes for you and your parents. If you disobey them, you will be inviting an appropriate punishment. But if you honor their feelings and rules, you will most likely enjoy a good relationship with them. You will of course occasionally make mistakes. Everyone does. But when you do, your sense of *responsibility* will help you own up to them. Surprisingly, doing so is the fastest way to put a wrong move behind you. It's also a terrific way to grow and improve as a person. The truth is, we grow the most from our mistakes—but only if we take *responsibility* for them.

responsibility in action

You are in a school play, but you haven't learned all your lines yet. There is a dress rehearsal tomorrow, but you have already agreed to meet your buddies this evening to play a game of soccer. You're stuck. If you play soccer, you'll let down your fellow actors. If you go to rehearsal, your soccer friends will be annoyed. What do you do?

Own up to your "wrong move." Call your soccer-playing friends and tell them with an apology that you made a mistake and explain why you can't play. Make it clear that you would really like to be there and that any night they choose next week would be fine with you. By doing this you will have fulfilled your most important *responsibility* and also given your friends a chance both to feel appreciated and to understand your predicament. Everyone makes mistakes. It's easier to forgive a person who admits to them.

You are sleeping over at a friend's house and suddenly one girl decides it would be fun to make mischievous phone calls. Others begin to make them and finally one friend calls out, "It's your turn!" You smile. It's harmless enough, you tell yourself. But for some reason you can't bring yourself to walk to the phone. What's wrong?

Wrong question. What's right is more like it. The answer is your sense of *responsibility*. Making mischievous phone calls doesn't feel right to you. Having received a few yourself, you know they can be anything from annoying to frightening. The problem is, you don't want to lose friends over the issue. The best thing to do is simply to state how you feel. "I don't want to do it. I think it bothers people. I'll just watch TV" would be fine. And if someone accuses you of being "chicken," don't rush to the phone to prove you're not sprouting feathers. Simply look your friend in the eye and say, "Absolutely not. I just don't think it's fun." Chances are you'll get more *respect* than teases, and that's a *savvy* way to handle a difficult situation.

2. compromise

"Let's both give a little so we can have what we want."

Have you ever made plans to go with a friend to the movies but were unable to agree on which film to see?
Have you ever disagreed with your parents over an allowance or curfew and stormed up to your room without finishing the discussion?
Have you ever refused to join a committee at school because the one you really wanted had enough members?
Do you fight endlessly with your siblings over who is going to watch what program?
Are your phone conversations often interrupted by another member of your family picking up the extension and saying, "Are you still on this thing?"
Have you ever gone out to a restaurant with a friend and ignored his or her remark that the menu was too expensive?

Compromise means giving a little to get a little. It means paying attention to what other people need or want and making an effort to accommodate them, while expressing your own needs too. Often this means you will have to put aside a desire of your own. That may be hard for you. But in deciding to do so you will have allowed everyone a chance to be a part of a decision. That always makes people feel good. *Compromise* is extremely savvy because it accomplishes many things. When people see that you are willing to *compromise*, they feel appreciated, understood, and liked. They may also feel more inclined to make you or the next person feel the same way.

compromise in action

You are at a spectacular party and no one is going home before 12:30 A.M. The problem is, you have a curfew of 11:30 P.M. Filled with apprehension, you call your parents, explain you're having a wonderful time, and ask if they would let you stay until the end. They say absolutely not. Now, is the evening over? Maybe not.

Try a *compromise*. Suggest something like, "Okay. Could I stay just a little longer? You name the time and I'll be home. I won't ask this every time. This is just special." They may or may not agree, and of course if they don't, you will be disappointed. Make sure you are home by 11:30 and then the next day start a discussion about pushing back your curfew just a little bit, pointing out you did exactly as they asked last night—as you usually do. You have proven you are responsible, and your parents will know that. Either now or in the future they will probably be more open to your requests.

You and your friend have just climbed onto a crowded bus after a long day of ice-skating. There is only one seat left and you are tempted to dive for it. You can see the same look in your friend's eye, but you are closer. "Well," you think to yourself, "is this a case of may the best man win?" Yes and no. It depends on how you define "win." To me, it's doing the right thing by both of you. So how can you do this with one seat?

Through *compromise*. Either try to share it or turn to your friend and say, "Well, the ride is fifteen minutes. Let's divide it up. Seven and a half minutes for you, and the rest for me." You may have to flip a coin to see who gets to sit first, but no matter what happens, both of you will have won. You didn't fight or act selfishly. You acknowledged each other's fatigue and were willing to compromise so each of you could rest. That's savvy. That's a good friendship.

3. sensitivity

"I want to be careful not to hurt your feelings."

Does your mind often wander while a friend is confiding his or her feelings to you?
When you are angry at your brother, do you tease him about the thing he is most sensitive about?

When you see a disabled person, do you stare?

When someone asks a question in class that you and your friends think is dumb, do you laugh?

Have you ever tried to butter up a very popular student at the expense of your friends?

When you become angry at one parent, do you find yourself telling him or her that you like the other parent better?

Sensitivity is perhaps the trickiest of all the building blocks because it requires that you consider not only what another person wants, but also how he or she feels. Since most feelings are invisible, this is not a simple thing. Putting oneself in someone else's shoes takes a lot of serious imagination. We all have our own lives and tend to get very caught up with the details. It isn't easy to stop and consider what another person might be feeling. But that is what *sensitivity* requires. You have to consider another person, aside and apart from yourself, and respond to that person with special caring for what's going on in his or her life.

Of course, being sensitive has its rewards. For one thing, it feels good to offer understanding to others. And secondly, people usually remember being treated thoughtfully. The next time you find yourself in a painful time, you will more than likely receive the same comforting attention—perhaps not from every friend to whom you have behaved sensitively but certainly a few. Remember, different friends are capable of different things.

sensitivity in action

You have just received an A on a math test for which you and your friend studied very hard. Thrilled, you approach your buddy, holding the test paper over your head like a trophy. But the look on his face makes it clear he didn't do nearly as well. Probably you would love to simply slink away. But nothing could be more hurtful to your friend. You are in this together.

Think sensitively. First, be sympathetic. "I guess you feel bad" would do nicely. Then think about what you would like to hear if you were in his shoes. More than likely it would be the comforting perspective that all is not lost and next time you might do better. So try that. "Look, it's only one test. Next time maybe we could study together for an hour or so and learn from each other." In this way not only will you be expressing your understanding of his feelings, but you will also be offering help in a sensitive way. You're not showing off. You're simply offering to help and suggesting the possibility that he could end up helping you too. If the tables were turned, wouldn't that make you feel good?

While walking down the street with a friend, you are stopped by a stranger with a very heavy accent. He is obviously trying to ask for directions, but you can't understand a word he is saying. Your friend is starting to laugh and the stranger is clearly growing upset and embarrassed. You feel horribly uncomfortable and very frustrated. You want to help, but you also want out because you can't figure out what to do.

Be savvy, apply a little *sensitivity*. First, imagine how you would feel. There you are in a foreign country, with an appointment to meet someone, only you can't figure out how to get there because no one can understand you. What would you want? Kindness and patience. You need to slow down and listen with a different ear. A more careful ear. It's important to communicate to this person that you are going to try to understand and that you don't think his struggle to speak is funny. In fact, he's doing quite well. This is easily accomplished by a warm smile, a soft voice, and, a motion of the hand to try again. Chances are in a moment or two this stranger will come up with a few understandable words and you will be able to help him. And remember, never shout in order to make yourself understood. This person speaks a foreign language. He isn't deaf.

*"**Y**ou have value as a person."*

Do you often break your parents' rules when they aren't looking?
Have you more than once let a friend's secret slip to other people?
Do you ever keep people waiting?
*Do you sometimes borrow things from your friends and then have to be re-
minded repeatedly to return them?*
Have you ever lent something that does not belong to you to a friend?
*Have you ever agreed with one friend and then turned around and voiced an
opposite opinion to another?*

Showing someone *respect* is the same thing as saying, "I think you have a right to be treated well." Once you accept this definition, it becomes clear that almost everyone you meet deserves *respect*. *Respect* can be expressed in all kinds of ways, not just through "please" and "thank you." When you refrain from interrupting someone else's conversation, you are showing *respect*. You are saying, "I think you deserve the right to finish talking. What you are saying is not necessarily less important than what I have to say." When you leave a few cookies in the jar so that other people in your family can enjoy them, you are showing *respect*. You are saying, "I think you all have a right to share in this nice thing." And when your friend tells you he or she doesn't want to talk about something upsetting and you change the subject, then you are showing *respect*. You are saying, "I care about your feelings, and you have a right to every last one of them."

respect in action

Your mother has just purchased an expensive cologne and has specifically told you not to go near it. But you are going out to a party tonight and you're dying to put some on. After all, how will she ever find out? She has left for the evening already. What, after all, is the harm?

The harm is in getting into the habit of not respecting what the other members of your family have asked of you. We all assume that our family members won't stop loving us. In most cases this is true. But we forget that family members can easily stop trusting, respecting, and relying on us. *That does not feel good.* So be savvy, and be *respect-ful.* Your mother has a right to keep that cologne to herself. And she has a right to expect that you will *respect* her wishes. Certainly you would expect the people around you to leave your new can of tennis balls or a new tape or a favorite sweater alone out of *respect* for *your* property. You must return the favor.

A substitute teacher has just entered the classroom and immediately the class begins to giggle and whisper. She introduces herself and then asks that everyone settle down. But they don't, yourself included. You'd like to stop, but something is making you too nervous to do so and you can tell that your friends feel the same way.

Whispering and giggling will usually have more to do with everyone's discomfort over a new authority figure than it will with their desire to annoy or tease her. But *respect* is something that needs to override your nervousness. Often when we are just having a good laugh, we forget it's at someone else's expense. *Respect*, however, requires that you come out of yourself a little so that you can say, "You're important too." Settling down is a way of respecting the teacher. It acknowledges that "we are your students and we want to hear what you have to say." Simply paying attention to what your teacher asks or says is the greatest *respect* you can pay her. And it's a very easy thing to do.

5. know-how

"No problem. I can do it!"

Have you ever been terrified in a fancy restaurant that you were eating with the wrong utensil?

When you're introduced to someone, do you immediately fall silent after saying "Hello"?

Have you ever unwrapped a gift in front of the giver and then had to say something nice, even though you hated it?

Have you ever been a guest at a dinner party only to realize you absolutely couldn't stand the main course?

Have you ever had food caught in your braces right at the beginning of the meal?

Have you ever tried to let others know you're good at something but ended up bragging instead?

When I speak of *know-how*, I am referring to the nuts and bolts of doing things with ease and style, the facts of social savvy. Having a little *know-how* will always convey some nice things about you. That you care how others see you, that you want others to feel comfortable, and that you can get what you want without stepping on other people's toes are only a few examples.

know-how in action

You are sitting at the dinner table with your family and your father's business clients. The conversation has turned to things you don't understand and you would like to leave the table. Usually, when it's just your family, you simply say, "May I please be excused?" But you sense this may not be enough right now.

You're right. Company does require something a little special. It's time for table manners *know-how*. Something like "May I please be excused? Dinner was great, but I have a lot of homework" is a fine example. It's polite, it compliments the hostess (your mother!), and it offers a good excuse for leaving the table. The dinner guests will feel respected and be understanding.

You have just gotten up to the cash register after eating a hamburger and french fries. You look down at the bill, take out your wallet, and stop. *The total seems too high and when you take a closer look, you notice that the hamburger price seems higher than the one indicated on the menu. The man at the cash register, however, is rushing you along by saying, "Are you paying or what?" You can feel yourself getting terribly nervous.*

Just consider a little restaurant *know-how!* Simply ask to see the menu by saying something like, "I think there might be a mistake on my bill. May I please see the menu to check a price?" Once you have received the menu, thank the cashier and if you are correct, calmly point it out to him. He will make the necessary adjustment. You will have acted very savvy by not having let your fear of being embarrassed stop you from checking your bill, which is your right.

Hopefully, by now you can see that social savvy is composed of a lot of interrelated parts: When you're *compromising*, you are showing *respect* and taking *responsibility* for yourself. When you're being *sensitive*, you are being not only *respectful*, but also *responsible*. And by doing all of these things gracefully, you are exhibiting your *know-how*. At home, at school, or out and about, a little social savvy will give you the confidence to make almost all the right moves. (No one does everything right all the time!)

It's time to begin applying all of this to very specific areas of your life.

conversations with ease

*T*here's no doubt about it. Talking looks easy. But sooner or later all of us come to realize it's a lot more complicated than it looks or sounds. Talking is something we all care about a great deal. It is a powerful way for most of us to communicate who we are. It's what we use to capture other people's affection, attention, and *respect*. And precisely because we attach so much importance to it, emotions play a key role in our ability to communicate. Some emotions, like sympathy or excitement, can actually help a conversation flow. But if you're feeling very nervous, it can be awfully difficult to have a nice "chat"!

This is not to say, of course, that emotions are the only things that muddy up a clear conversation. Shaky communication skills can cause a lot of trouble as well. Unfortunately, most of us are not aware of our weaknesses in this area. After all, we do have some skills. We know, for example, that it's not polite to interrupt or to point and laugh. We know when to say hello, thank you, excuse me, and good-bye and when to introduce one person to another. We easily carry on in-depth conversations with close friends. But there is a whole lot more to good conversation skills than just the simple basics.

The truth is, I can't do much about your nervousness in approaching a new person, but I can help you feel a bit more confident that you will have things to say. I can't keep you from forgetting a few people's names, but I can show you how to get through the awkward period of not remembering with a smile. And I can't keep the hurt away if someone is clearly not listening to a thing you have to say. But I can suggest a few ways to walk away that will save you from any more bad feelings.

A person with good communication skills is a person with a good deal of savvy. He or she will feel confident in almost any social situation. So let's take a careful look at how to improve your conversation techniques, cope with the classic awkward or unsettling moments that might crop up, and even overcome the special problems the telephone presents! Learn to express yourself. It's the only way for others to discover how special you are.

what is a good conversation?

Before we explore how to start, stay in, and leave a good conversation, I think it might be a good idea to take a look at the elements of a good conversation.

• There is a positive start with eye contact, a smile, and sometimes a firm handshake.

• Each person listens carefully to the other.

• Each person expresses interest in the other.

• Each person feels appreciated.

• Neither person feels he or she is giving more than he or she is getting.

• Both people feel their views are being respected.

• Each person walks away feeling he or she said what he or she had to say.

And perhaps most important, a good conversation is one in which each person knows how to "volleyball"—both people give each other something to respond to so that thoughts can continually flow. So, how do we get there? Let's take a look at the basics first, and then we'll move to the details.

body language: body talk

Saying what you mean is not enough. You also have to look as if you mean what you say. Otherwise, your words will not be trusted. Interest is not something you convey by simply being there and talking. It's something that you communicate with your whole being. Here are a number of tips to help you convey your openness to, and interest in, a good conversation.

• *Don't* fold your arms across your chest. That stance says to people, "I'm holding back. I have a secret."

• *Do* let your arms rest gently at your sides. If you need a prop like a soda can or book to hold on to, fine. A relaxed body says, "I feel good. This is nice."

• *Don't* stand with your shoulders hunched. That says, "I have so many problems, I don't know what to do." No one wants to talk to someone who looks overburdened already. Besides, it puts too much strain on your back and it's not good for your posture.

• *Do* allow your shoulders to relax, and if you want to be approached, turn your head from side to side slightly as if you are looking around. That says, "I'm open to you."

• *Don't* stand stiffly with both legs stick-straight. All that seems to say is, "I'm not relaxed. I'm stuck." That will leave your partner feeling very uneasy. It's simply not inviting.

• *Do* occasionally, as you are talking, allow your weight to shift from foot to foot. You won't look restless if you keep your eyes basically on the person with whom you are talking. Finding a comfortable position says, "I want to be here."

• *Don't* lean backward in a thoughtful stance. It will seem judgmental, as if you were saying, "Hmmmm, now what do I think of you." It may also cause your partner to suspect he or she has bad breath.

• *Do* lean in occasionally as you and your partner are talking. That says, "I am really interested in what we are talking about and I don't want to miss a thing."

• *Don't* look deadly serious every moment, even if you are talking about a somber subject. Your partner could think you are bored, annoyed, or unhappy. Sympathetic looks and knowing soft smiles can also say, "I'm taking this conversation seriously."

• *Do* smile and nod occasionally. Smiles make everyone feel good.

Almost unconsciously, people translate a smile into meaning "I like you" or "I approve of what you are saying" or "I feel understood" or "This is fun." A nod, with or without a smile, also signals understanding and approval. That would inspire anyone to keep talking!

• *Don't* let your eyes wander too often from the person you are speaking with, even if it's because you feel shy or embarrassed. He or she will conclude you are bored, thinking of other things, more interested in other people, or simply self-involved. Drifting eyes say, "I'd rather be doing something else."

• *Do* make eye contact. Focus on your partner's face. It's a way of saying, "I am interested in what you are saying, not in what is going on around me." Of course, occasionally you may want to look over his or her shoulder or down at the floor (never check your watch!), but that is something both of you need. No one likes to be stared at nonstop. That can feel too intense. And you certainly can't enjoy looking at the same place every moment. It could make you bug-eyed!

listening and asking questions

Asking questions is a terrific way of saying, "I am interested in you. I want to hear what you have to say." This will of course make your partner feel wonderful. It does not follow, however, that you can just throw out any old question. And that's where the *listening* part comes in. During the course of a conversation, you will get lots of clues: clues that tell you what your partner is interested in, clues about his or her day, and clues about his or her life. That is why listening is critical. You will want to use what you discover as a basis for what I call your *safe* questions.

the art of asking safe questions

There is a true art to asking good, safe conversational questions. A good question draws people out. It offers them a choice of how much and what they might say. And a good question is also savvy because it will help your partner think of things to ask you, so the conversation can keep going! Here are some guidelines I always follow in my efforts to pose good, safe questions.

• If it's someone you hardly know, take a cue from what they are wearing or carrying. A person holding a tennis racket might inspire you to ask, "That's a nice racket. Do you play a lot of tennis?" This is a safe start because this person has chosen to be seen with tennis gear. Chances are he or she will be happy to talk about it.

• Always try to ask a question that safely inspires more than just a one-word answer such as yes or no. "What's your favorite color?" for instance, is a dead end. All it requires is a one-word answer, and if two people are nervous talking together, the entire conversation might stop right there. After all, what do you say next? "What do you own that's red?" Instead, try something like, "I love this kind of music. Rock pop is my favorite.

You are standing at a party talking with someone whose eyes keep darting around the room. He looks terribly uninterested in everything you are saying. Though he is making a small effort at conversation, you can tell he's not listening to you. You feel dreadful and want to excuse yourself.

Try to direct your bad feelings away from yourself and more toward your partner, who is apparently being very rude. Then consider what might be going on. He could be one of those people who is afraid of missing anything. He may also be someone who gets nervous talking to anyone at any length. Or he could simply be more interested in something or someone else. The point is, it's his problem. He should learn how to gracefully disengage himself from the conversation when the mood to wander hits. But since he hasn't, it's up to you to step away. At the first pause, smile quickly and say, "You know, I see someone over there I know. Would you excuse me, please?" or "Umm, I think I'll go and get something to eat. Please excuse me," and then with a quick "good-bye" walk away.

You are in the middle of your first conversation with a person who seems interesting enough. But now, all of a sudden she shares something you feel is too personal. In fact, you feel embarrassed. She tells you her parents fight very loudly all the time. You wouldn't feel uncomfortable if it were an old friend, but with someone new it's different—and you'd rather not go on with this type of conversation.

When someone draws us too close too fast, it is a nat-ural response to want to pull back. The only thing is, when a person does reveal so much, it's usually because he or she feels very needy or very lonely. It's more important than ever to be gentle and sensitive in our response. Still, there's no reason to have to stay in a conversation that is making you dreadfully un-comfortable. The goal here is to move out of the one you're in with care. When your part-ner pauses, simply say, "That must make you feel awful."

Smile at her sympathetically and then say something like, "But look, we're here now. This isn't a bad party! Why don't we get something to munch on?" By doing this you will have let her know you heard what she had to say and that you understood her emotions. That will feel good to her. But at the same time you will be allowing yourself to step away from a conver-sation you are simply not ready for. That will make both of you feel good.

What do you like best?" It's true the answer to this might be one word, like, "Classical." But then there are loads of follow-up questions you could ask. "Do you play or just listen?" "What are your favorite recordings?" and "Have you been to any concerts?" are just a few.

• Ask questions that would invite your partner to discuss something more personal but would not require that he or she do so. "Do you have any brothers or sisters?" is a good example. Your partner can answer yes or no without having to divulge anything about his or her relationship with them—and yet still find things to say, such as their ages or where they go to school.

• Ask questions that explore where the two of you might have some common ground. Usually these work best when you start with a state-ment about yourself as a kind of springboard—and then dive off with a related question about the other person. For example: "I just went skiing. I love the feeling of rushing down a mountain. Are you into winter sports?" Or, "I'm so nervous about my part in the school play. I've been working so hard on it! Do you ever get nervous when you have to get up and speak?" The idea here is to let your partner know something about you and to invite him or her to talk more openly. This usually works beautifully.

avoiding dangerous questions

Dangerous questions are those that have the potential of hurting or angering your partner. Everyone has uttered one or two of these. If you're talking to someone you don't know very well, it's easy to ask a question that could upset them. After all, you don't know their sensitive spots yet. When this happens, the best thing to do is to face it. "I'm sorry. I see I upset you. I didn't mean to. I hope you will forgive me" is the best way to go. It will show your partner you care, which always helps.

However, most times you can avoid asking the wrong thing—as long as you stick to these rules.

• *Don't* ask a question you wouldn't want to answer. If it would make you feel awkward or embarrassed, you can bet it might do the same to your partner.

• *Don't* ask about something negative you've heard or can see about this person. "Did you really almost fail the math test?" will never do. Your partner will be stuck having to fess up to something painful he or she may not want to talk about. Other examples of this kind of question (no matter how sympathetically you say them) are "Where did you get that limp?" "Did you really get kicked off the baseball team?" and "Are you slightly cross-eyed?"

• *Don't* let your questions get too personal if it's someone you hardly know. "Is it true your parents are divorced? You must feel terrible" is not smart. Neither is "Do you and your brother have a lot in common?" Again, you will be forcing someone who could be in a lot of pain to think and talk about something they may not want to concentrate on—least of all with a new friend! Also, most people are uncomfortable with those who try to get too close too fast. Other examples of this kind of question (no matter how well intentioned) are "Does your mother *have* to work?" "Why don't your parents ever send you to camp?" "Your father looks sick. Why?" and "That's a great wallet. Didn't that cost a lot?"

• *Don't* ask, "What else is new?" This kind of question is much too challenging. It's like saying to a person, "Come on now. Entertain me." That's very unfair to your partner, who will likely feel horrified that he or she can't think of a thing to say. Few people could under such pressure!

• *Don't* ask questions unrelated to the point your partner is making just because you have something else on your mind. All that will do is say to your partner, "I only care about what I want to say. Let's change the subject. Your point doesn't count." If your partner has just told you that he or she missed a great shot during a tennis match and feels terrible, don't say, "I've always wanted to try out for the tennis team. Whom do I speak to?" Your partner may want to talk a moment about his or her feelings or situation, but you are attempting to continue the conversation by focusing only on yours. Your partner needs time and it is your *responsibility* to give it. Then it will be your turn. It has to do with balance, which brings us to my next point.

no hiding

Conversations need the involvement of two people. Each person has to listen and talk. Each person has to share thoughts and ideas. Each person has to give and get—maybe not in totally equal amounts—but close enough so that no one feels cheated ("I told her a lot about me, but she barely told me a thing") or embarrassed ("All I did was talk about me. Maybe I confided too much").

It's true that most people like to talk about themselves. We've already discussed the importance of making others feel you are interested in them. But now let's look at it from another angle. No conversation can feel satisfying unless both people feel as if they have shared something.

In a conversation this means allowing people to know you as you would like to know them. If someone says to you, "I'm very good in English and history, but I have so many problems with math," it's not fair to reply simply "Why?" and then once they answer, change the subject. Rather, you need to discuss what troubles your partner the most and then *share* the subjects that cause you concern. This sharing does not apply, however, to a conversation in which someone has confided something deeply personal. You are then not obligated to share your own secret. It is simply your *responsibility* to listen.

Conversations are not mathematical things. We don't, nor should we, sit around counting words to make sure each of us has equal time. But we do need to "sense" a balance. We need to pay attention to what's being said and what part of ourselves we can bring to the conversation. An entire conversation can be built around a difficulty your friend is having with his or her mother, but it will be a balanced experience if you both talk, listen, and share feelings.

Okay, now we are ready to look at the finer points of making conversation with confidence.

saying hello and a bit of small talk

The goal of an introduction is for two people to learn each other's name and perhaps one significant detail about the other so that a conversation can take place. The goal of small talk is to have a light, pleasant talk with someone you are not very close with or hardly know. Greeting someone for the first time, then, is connected to making small talk, since without a greeting there would be no conversation. Here are some introduction pointers.

• If you are the one introducing two people, it is your responsibility to mention a subject about which they can chat. For instance: "Bill, I'd like you to meet Steve. Steve just got back from a camping trip in the mountains." Or, "Pamela, this is my friend Kathleen. Kathleen, this is my friend Pamela. Guess what you have in common? Being nuts about Madonna!" Or, "David, I'd like you to meet Candy. Candy, this is David, the one I told you about being a computer whiz."

miserable moment

You are at a party talking with a person who has just introduced himself. Now a friend walks over and is waiting for an introduction to your new acquaintance, only you've forgotten the new person's name. You feel incredibly embarrassed because it's clear they're waiting for you to do something.

So go ahead! Do something. If you stand there in silence, both of your friends might think you don't want to introduce them to each other or, worse, that you are being quite thoughtless. So, try the truth! Simply smile apologetically at your new acquaintance and say, "I'd like to introduce you to my friend Jim, but for the moment I've forgotten your name. I'm very sorry." True, your friend Jim could take it upon himself to say, "Hi, I'm Jim. What's your name," instead of waiting for you to do the introductions. But it's much nicer to take responsibility for your small weakness and to face the situation with a sense of humor. Everyone will feel a lot better and conversation is bound to flow.

- A man or a boy is always presented to a woman or a girl. "Mr. James, I would like you to meet Ms. Lee."
- It's always important to shake someone's hand. A firm one (coupled with a smile and eye contact) is best, but do remember that older people may suffer from arthritic hands. It could be painful for them to shake. If you know this in advance, offer only a verbal greeting.
- Kissing is not necessary unless it's a custom with your family, a European guest, or the wish of a relative. And always offer or kiss on the cheek. (Occasions, too, will dictate whether or not you kiss. Family gatherings, weddings, and small dinner parties usually inspire quite a bit of kissing.)
- When you introduce someone to another person, always say the older person's name first. "Mrs. Stuart, I'd like you to meet Dave."
- When you are introduced to someone, repeat their name. It's a good way to be sure you'll remember. For example, if someone says, "Beverly, I'd like you to meet Margaret," you might say, "Hello, Margaret. It's nice to meet you."
- If you did not clearly hear the name of the person you were just

introduced to, lean forward and say, "I'm sorry. I don't think I heard your name correctly. Could you please repeat it?" He or she will feel quite pleased you want to get it right.

• A young person should stand up when an adult walks into the room. It expresses *respect*.

• If you are about to meet the President of the United States or a dignitary of any sort, don't say a thing until you are spoken to! An aide will do the introductions. And you will respond, "How do you do, Mr. President. It's an honor to meet you." And don't try to make small talk unless he invites it. Chances are he has lots of other people to meet!

Now let's take a look at a few conversation openers. Suppose you have just been introduced to Sally. Here are a few things you might immediately say: "It's a pleasure to meet you." (Pause.) "What school do you go to?" Or, "I've heard a lot of neat things about you. Jill says you are a wonderful tennis player." Or, "It's nice to meet you." (Pause.) "This is a noisy party, isn't it!"

Now consider what these greetings will accomplish. First you offer a standard friendly greeting, which will convey how nice it is to be speaking to this new person. Then you follow up with a safe question, a compliment, and an observation—all of which point the way to a bit of small talk.

small talk

I said before that small talk is very closely linked to greetings. So let's listen to a sample small talk conversation that comes on the heels of an introduction. Notice it uses all the basic rules of a good conversation, but in a very limited way. By that I mean it doesn't try to do too much. The talk is light, safe, and impersonal.

> *"It's a pleasure to meet you. What school do you go to?"*
> *"Williston. It's a small private school three towns over."*
> *"Oh, I think I've heard of it. Don't you have a great tennis team?"*

"Actually, yes. I'm not on it, though. I play other sports."

"Really? Which ones?"

"Oh, soccer mostly . . ."

"Then you must have seen that game on TV last night! Incredible, huh?"

"You bet. Weren't you amazed when . . ."

Get the picture? It's light. Each person picks up on what the other is saying. (Yes, they are "volleyballing" while they are talking soccer!) No one gets too personal, but each is expressing interest in the other. So what's next?

---

class quote

"Miss Judith," someone whispered to me, "I'm always a little afraid to introduce two friends to each other because I'm afraid they'll like each other better than me." I smiled sympathetically. "I can understand having that thought," I replied. "It's true your friends may grow to like each other. After all, they have something wonderful in common—you! But whether or not they do become close friends has nothing to do with your friendship with either person. Your friendships will be what they are meant to be, no matter whom you 'introduce' into the picture."

---

the art of keeping a conversation in motion (despite some odds!)

Listening carefully, asking good questions, using body language, and sharing yourself are all necessary to keep a conversation going. But during the course of an extended talk, a lot of tricky things can happen. In fact, handled carelessly, the entire conversation could come to a grinding halt. Here is a look at the most commonly mishandled elements of a conversation and what to do about them.

silences

Silences can intrude on any conversation. No matter how lively or interesting the talk, a moment may arrive in which there seems to be nothing else to say. Sometimes it's merely a lull in the conversation, a kind of pause between thoughts when both people are trying to put their ideas together. Other times it signals that a topic of conversation has run out and that something new is needed. And many times a silence is something that occurs when two people are nervous and simply can't think of what to say.

The hardest thing to do when a silence occurs is to relax and let it happen. For some reason a silence often leads each person to conclude the other will think he or she is boring or dumb. Wrong! During a silence, most people are too busy blaming it on themselves to think about you! True, a silence will occasionally mean that two people are simply not on the same wavelength. But most times a silence may be happening because the moment has come to rest, think, and gather one's thoughts. For this reason it's important not to let panic set in. Chances are if you stay relaxed, another subject will naturally come up. Allowing for this cycle of conversation is one of the best ways to ensure that a fun give-and-take will continue—in a moment.

m i s e r a b l e

m o m e n t

You are sitting talking to a friend of your father's. You are feeling a little uncomfortable because talking to adults makes you nervous. In an effort to make some conversation, this nice man says, "So, do you like school?" You say yes and then suddenly realize you can't think of what else to say.

Contrary to what you might do with a person your age, which would then be to try to draw him or her out, this is a time for you to draw yourself out. So, give yourself a "pop" quiz! Why did you answer yes? What specifically do you like about school? Which subjects are your favorites? What about your classmates? Is there a group that does everything together? Do you enjoy playing sports? Now, just volunteer an answer. After you say yes, pause to quiz yourself and then speak up! Try, "I really like studying math and science," or "I especially like being on the debate team," or even, "But what I really like is being on the baseball team!" Now you will be helping this adult understand the things that are important to you. He will more than likely want to know more, and before you know it, you'll be talking!

o
m
e
n
t

You walk into a room where all your friends are standing and whispering. When they see you enter, they all stop talking.

You feel awful. Anyone would. After all, you are probably concluding that they were talking about you, or discussing something they don't want you to know about. Still, you're stuck. You can't run out. And you can't pretend you didn't notice. So what do you do? You get

brave. You walk up to your friends, smile at everyone, and say, "Am I interrupting anything?" or "Is this private?" Chances are if they are your friends, they will include you. Sometimes people who are discussing something personal or "secret" will stop talking the moment anyone walks into the room, even though they're not trying to exclude them. They're in a "private mode." You simply have to jolt them out of it.

Note: If this happens with a group of people you're not so friendly with, try something else. The moment you walk in and sense the problem, smile broadly and say, "Oh, excuse me. I didn't mean to interrupt." Then walk out. You won't feel great, but you will feel strong. You didn't allow them to intimidate you. That's called taking control! That's savvy.

However, if staying calm is impossible for you, or if you sense that the topic has been completely covered, then during the silence, look around. Comment on something about your surroundings. Mention something you're excited or concerned about that will be happening this week or next. In other words, make an effort to start fresh.

And if you can't relax enough to either let a silence happen or cleverly change the subject, then say so. "Boy, I feel real funny when I can't think of anything to say" is perfectly fine. Sometimes admitting to a difficult feeling can get rid of the tension. It can also serve to inspire a very interesting conversation!

One final note: People often resort to flattery or compliments, especially during silences. Compliments are a savvy way to begin a conversation. They can also be a positive way to change a subject or fill a lull. After all, they feel good. Unfortunately, they have a funny way of ringing false and thus making the person to whom they are directed feel as if they were being teased. So, please be truthful. If your friend is wearing an old faded cotton sweater, don't exclaim, "What a beautiful sweater you have on!" Instead, try, "That looks like a very comfortable sweater! You must love wearing it." If your friend has given you a gift you don't really like, don't exclaim, "Wow! This is spectacular! Where did you get it?" Try, "Oh, a present! Thanks for taking the time to pick it out."

And at all costs avoid what I call the "continuous compliment." This is one that doesn't stop. It jumps from subject to subject and usually comes from people who are terrified they will have nothing to say. Trouble is, in short order they won't have to worry. No one will want to talk with them anyway. Most people can sense the basic truth. Your friend knows her sweater isn't cover girl material. And chances are the gift you received is not the Taj Mahal. No need to act as if it were. Compliments should be used to inspire good feelings—not doubts.

hitting a nerve

It happens to everyone. Sooner or later we all say the wrong thing. And by "wrong" I mean something that hurts or upsets your particular partner. In general, it may not be an insensitive thing to say, but for this person it is painful. The moment it's out of your mouth you can tell something is wrong. Your partner falls instantly and angrily silent, snaps something back at you, or says, "That was mean." The temptation in moments like this is to run. But that will never work. Leaving a horrible moment hanging will bother you for days. Resolving it on the spot will help to put it out of your mind and keep it from spiraling into an argument.

My advice is face the blunder. Don't torture yourself about it. Don't feel guilty. It was an innocent mistake. Anyone could have made it. Still, it *was* a mistake. The *sensitive* and *respectful* thing to do would be to promptly say something like "I'm sorry. I didn't realize that would upset you" or "I feel terrible. I didn't mean to hurt you." This will show you care. Your partner, in turn, won't feel so bad because receiving someone else's warmth and concern always feels good.

when you don't agree

Conversations should never come to a grinding halt over a disagreement. But often they do. This is largely because most people don't know how to disagree. Some stubbornly state their opinion, insist they are right, assure the other person he or she is being silly or dumb, and then feel surprised when they have a fight on their hands. Others, afraid of an argument, say they agree when they really don't and then, because they are not telling the truth, find themselves in a very stilted and awkward conversation that soon ends. "What happened?" they think. "I didn't cause a fuss!"

Disagreements are as natural as rain. They can sometimes even be interesting! Here are some savvy guidelines on how to manage them.

• Be honest. State your opinion, but not as fact. "I feel . . ." or "In my opinion . . ." is the way to go. That way you won't sound like a know-it-all. You simply know how *you* feel. No one will get offended at that.

• Listen carefully to what your partner is saying and don't interrupt. He or she has the same right as you to express an opinion.

• Avoid making judgmental remarks no matter how tempted you are to blurt them out. "I can't believe you mean that!" or "That's the silliest thing I ever heard" or "That's ridiculous" will do nothing but quite understandably enrage your partner.

• When your partner is through, explain why you think he or she is wrong, using expressions like "Well, I disagree because. . . " or "I don't think that's true because . . ." or "I don't feel that way one bit. After all . . ." It's a very *respectful* way of letting someone know they have a right to their feelings but you disagree.

• Don't expect to agree after you have disagreed. Sometimes you will want to *compromise.* "I finally see what you mean, but surely you can see why I . . ." Other times you may simply have to respect each other's opinions and let it go. "I don't agree, but I still think of you as my friend." Disagreements don't mean you shouldn't be friends or that you have nothing in common. In fact, they mean quite the opposite.

Two friends gain the most from each other when they bring different thoughts and feelings to the relationship. They learn from each other. They make each other think. So when disagreements spring up, go with them! It may be an opportunity to learn something!

expressing anger

Anger is a very difficult emotion to express. This is true largely because it can be so overwhelming. It can influence the way you see everything and make you lose sight of reason. It can force you to lose control of yourself and further confuse the situation. And it can feel just plain awful. But, and this is a big but, it doesn't have to.

Anger is a natural emotion. You simply need to control it instead of the other way around. Expressing anger carefully is very important. Here are some basic guidelines.

• Find a period of time during which you can really talk it out with your friend. Rushing isn't good. Nor is having to stop an angry conversation in the middle. Pick a time when you can really focus together.
• Before speaking, take a few deep breaths. Feel the tension leave your body. Doing this will help you gain some control over your emotions.
• If you are angered by something someone has done, first ask them why or how it happened. This is critical, because sometimes we may misunderstand a situation. We may not know all the details, which would clarify why a hurtful situation arose. Give your friend a chance to explain.
• If the explanation is not satisfactory, don't attack. That will only put your friend on the defensive, making it impossible for him or her to hear *you* out. Instead, remember to couple whatever you have to say that is negative with something positive. For instance, "You have been such a good friend. Why did you do this?"
• As your friend continues to explain his or her position, *really listen.*

Don't just concentrate on your own negative feelings. Even if you are still angry with your friend, you might find out something that will help you understand him or her a little better. That can only serve to improve your friendship.

• Never leave the conversation hanging. It's fine for each of you to part still feeling angry at each other. But it isn't okay to part not knowing where you go from here. Will you talk again tonight? Tomorrow? Do you still want to be friends? Do you each need a little time to cool off? Establish what you're going to do at the end of the conversation. It's cruel for either one of you to keep the other one in a state of limbo.

If you are the one with whom someone is angry, there are definitely a few additional things you need to keep in mind.

• Hear your friend out. Don't interrupt with defensive remarks like "That's not true!" or "You have no right to say that!" He or she has the same right as you to be heard—even if he or she is wrong.

• If you think your friend is wrong to be angry with you, don't be afraid to stick up for yourself. But do acknowledge his or her feelings. "I can see you are really upset and I'm sorry, but I'm not to blame" is one example. Pretending you think you're wrong just to keep the peace will never work. That will end up making you feel angry, and sooner or later you'll get into another unpleasant confrontation.

• If you are wrong, just admit it. It's a lot easier to forgive someone who fesses up to their mistakes than it is someone who refuses to accept responsibility for them. Saying you're sorry takes a lot of strength. It is also an expression of *respect*. Your friend will appreciate that you were willing to acknowledge an error. It is a way of saying you honor the friendship.

Face-to-face conversations are not the only ones that require social savvy. Many conversations may happen over the phone . . . and they require some very special *know-how*.

the art of good telephone conversation

The telephone is a handy and pleasant way to communicate. It feels good to just pick up the receiver, dial a number, and share a feeling or piece of news. But talking on the telephone is not always a simple matter. There are communication issues the phone introduces that are not present in face-to-face greetings or conversations. Still, there is good news! Strong telephone skills can be *easily* learned.

incoming calls

There are a number of things to keep in mind when that phone rings.

- Answer the phone with a pleasant voice. That way the caller will feel welcome. Remember, when you answer the phone, you are representing your family.
- If the caller wants to speak to your parent or sibling, don't just put the phone down and call their name. Instead say, "Just one moment, please. I'll see if she's available," or, "Please hold on. I'll tell her you're on the phone." Otherwise the caller may feel stranded or unsure you've heard him or her correctly.
- If the person the caller wishes to speak to is not home, you will need to take a careful message. If you are unsure of the spelling of the caller's name, ask. Always repeat the phone number that is given to you, to make sure you have written it down correctly.
- Do ask the caller if there is any message. Sometimes people would like to leave one but don't want to bother the person answering the phone.
- If someone is calling at a bad time, say so. Don't pretend you're listening when you aren't. He or she will not be fooled, and it will hurt a lot. It's much better to say, "May I call you back? I'm in the middle of doing something. What's a good time?" That way you'll avoid calling him or her at an awkward moment!
- If the call is for you but someone else in the house needs to use the

phone, say so. Don't rush off saying, "I can't talk now," or, "I've got to get off." Remember to explain. "May I call you back? My father is waiting for an important call" is a good example.

• If it's a call for you but you don't want to speak to the caller, try not to be abrupt. The goal is always, no matter whom you are with or *how* you are with them, to be *sensitive* and *respectful*. Rushing off the phone would make the caller feel awful. It won't hurt to say hello, make a bit of small talk for a moment, such as, "What did you think of the math test?" and then a minute or so later, during a pause, say, "Thanks for calling, but you know, I have a lot of homework! I really should get off and do it." The other person won't feel great, but he or she won't feel insulted either. That's savvy.

outgoing calls

Most of us are not mind readers. We have no idea what's going on in someone else's home when we decide to call them. You need to be prepared!

• If the person you are calling does not answer the phone, then no matter how urgently you would like to reach him or her, take the time to politely speak to whoever answers. If your friend's parent picks up the phone, introduce yourself and then ask for your friend. "Hello, Mrs. Morgan. This is John. May I please speak with Tim?" Remember to say thank you when his mother or father says "hold on."
• If when your call is picked up you can hear a lot of noise on the other end, you might want to say, "Sounds like you're busy. Is this a good time to talk?" That way you will help your friend communicate whether or not he or she can really talk and save yourself from the hurt of speaking to someone who isn't really listening.
• If you accidentally dial the wrong number, never say, when an unfamiliar voice answers, "Who's this?" It's none of your business! Instead, either ask to speak to your friend, since the person answering could be a visitor, or say, "Is this 555-2100?" If it isn't, apologize and hang up.

Okay. Now you're on the phone with your friend, and in the middle of an involved conversation. Here are some things to keep in mind.

• You can't see your partner's face and he or she can't see yours. If you say something seriously but there's a smile on your face to indicate you're teasing, how will your partner know? All he or she hears is your somber tone of voice. When you're on the phone, you need to express *as precisely as possible* what you are feeling.

• You can't see your partner's body language nor can he or she see yours. Therefore neither of you can really tell if the other is listening, bored, or interested in other things. All you have to go on is the nature of the responses you hear as you are talking. A lot of "uh-huhs" may work in person with lots of eye contact but not on the phone. They usually sound as if the person were really saying, "I can't wait for this conversation to be over." Remember, phrases such as "I see what you mean" or "I understand what you are saying" are helpful. So is interjecting specific remarks to prove you are listening, such as "I agree, but I don't think . . ." or "I don't understand; could you explain . . ." These comments prove you are listening and caring.

• When you want to get off the phone, use as much grace as you would if you were talking in person. Wait for a pause and then warmly say something like, "It was really nice talking to you, but I promised my dad I'd help him with something." You might even say, if you're very comfortable with this person, "Honestly, I'm all talked out now!"

• People often cannot speak freely when there are others around. Trouble is, the caller won't know if your sibling is near. If you can't answer a question openly, make it clear by saying, "Can we talk about that later? It's not a good time." Otherwise your stiff answers might make you sound angry or bored.

Being a good conversationalist is a wonderful thing. Happily, there is no one way to do that. Everyone brings their own personality to the task. But there are some basic communication skills that will go a long way toward helping you express yourself clearly and positively. It is extremely *sensitive* and *respectful* to say what you mean and listen carefully to others, leaving them feeling understood and appreciated. *Compromising* so that others have a chance to express themselves and taking *responsibility* for "volleyballing" will further any conversation. And a bit of *know-how* (the final building block), such as basic phone savvy or introduction pointers, will help you each time you have something to say.

friendships and how to keep them

Everyone needs friends. Friendship offers an opportunity to share experiences. It's a chance to give and receive comfort, understanding, and *sensitivity*. A friend can help you understand something new about the world and even help you learn interesting things about yourself. For all of these reasons, most people want friends. Trouble is, not everyone knows how to be a good one.

Most friendships happen naturally. Two people meet, find they have things in common, and begin spending time together. Trust grows and confidences are shared. Happy, sad, and difficult times arise and yet the friendship continues, growing stronger with each new experience.

But it isn't always easy. And that's where friendship savvy comes in. Certainly everything you learned in Chapter Two will help to strengthen your friendships, but now let's take it a step further. Let's explore the true meaning of friendship and how one can give it the *respect* it deserves. Once you understand that, you're bound to be a very savvy (and caring!) friend.

keeping tabs on your friendship skills

There is no question that people become friends not just because they laugh at the same things or have the same interests or even think alike. People also become friends because for some mysterious reason they just seem to understand and appreciate each other. The word "chemistry" is often used to describe this attraction because it suggests that a friendship is based not only on what we say or do, but also on how we *react* to each other. Everyone has friends that are in many ways different from themselves but who still make them feel good when they're together. Well, that's "chemistry." The trouble sets in, however, when people rely too much on their chemistry to keep a friendship going.

Friendships need attention. They cannot be left to fend for themselves. Some people would say friendships need "work." I prefer not to use that word. I like "attention" instead. I believe the qualities one brings to a friendship can be pleasurable for everyone.

Below is an inventory of skills necessary for a good friendship that I have designed for a dual purpose: one, to help you focus on some of the most important qualities of a solid friendship; and two, to give you an opportunity to see how often you offer these qualities in your own friendships. (After you have completed the inventory, we will go back and explore these qualities more deeply.) Give yourself: 0 points for "Rarely"; 1 point for "Usually"; and 2 points for "Almost always."

the friendship skill inventory

• *Acceptance:* Do you allow your friends to have their own opinions, make their own decisions, and disagree with you?

       Rarely   Usually   Almost always

• *Patience:* Do you allow your friends to talk about themselves when they are upset, even though you'd rather discuss something else?

       Rarely   Usually   Almost always

• *Noncompetitiveness:* Can you compliment your friends even though you are feeling bad about yourself?

       Rarely   Usually   Almost always

• *Trust:* Do you control the urge to let out a secret or to talk behind a friend's back?

       Rarely   Usually   Almost always

• *Thoughtfulness:* Do you think about a problem a friend is having even when he or she is not discussing it with you?

Rarely   Usually   Almost always

• *Honesty:* If a good friend asks you a question, do you tell him or her the truth instead of what you think he or she wants to hear?

Rarely   Usually   Almost always

• *Sacrifice:* Have you ever done something nice for a friend even though it meant not doing something for yourself?

Rarely   Usually   Almost always

• *Sharing:* Do you invite your friends to enjoy your good fortune, be it a terrific dessert or a great book?

Rarely   Usually   Almost always

• *Understanding:* When a friend is upset about a problem and snaps at you unfairly, do you let the remark pass?

Rarely   Usually   Almost always

• *Sensitivity:* If a friend is describing a situation that made him or her feel bad, do you keep your own good news to yourself?

Rarely   Usually   Almost always

• *Reliability:* If you say you are going to meet a friend at a particular place and time, do you?

Rarely   Usually   Almost always

• *Strength:* If your friend is going through a hard time, are you able to stick by his or her side, knowing it's not going to be a lot of fun?

Rarely   Usually   Almost always

• *Compromise:* Are you able to put off your desire to enjoy one activity when your friends are in the mood to do something else?

Rarely   Usually   Almost always

• *Loyalty:* If a very popular person starts paying attention to you, do your old friends still seem more important?

Rarely   Usually   Almost always

Score _____

If you scored 21–28, you are a very talented friend. Still, nobody's perfect! Keep paying attention!

If you scored 14–20, you're a good friend, but there are some areas that could get you into trouble.

If you scored less than 14, you need to start paying lots more attention to the people you care about.

The above inventory should give you an idea of where you stand on friendship skill and the specific areas in which you might need to improve. No one, or rather no honest person, is going to circle "almost always" every time. The one thing that is *always* true is that we need to keep bringing as much of our good selves to a friendship as we can —and that some days we'll do better than others. What counts is the whole picture, not an occasional blunder. And if that occasional blunder does seem to lose you a friend or two . . . well, it is my opinion that if your apology was not accepted, then it wasn't such a great friendship anyway.

Now let's explore each of the qualities in the above inventory and what it means to a friendship.

acceptance

Friends need to accept each other. People need to know that even if they don't think a certain joke is funny, or don't come in first on the fifty-yard sprint, or aren't allowed to meet friends on a weeknight, they will still be liked. This doesn't mean you can't be disappointed. Absolutely you can. But a good friend doesn't try to *change* another. No two friends can think or act alike. Your friend can only be who he or she is. If you don't *respect* this fact, the friendship won't last.

patience

Friends need to allow each other to be, well, annoying! It's tempting to simply "tune out" when an upset or excited friend keeps going on and on about something. It's even easier to get annoyed at a friend who continually ignores your advice and keeps getting into trouble at

o   *Your friend has just invited you over to admire her new outfit. Quickly she slips it on for you and much to your dismay you can see that it looks awful. "What do you think?" she asks as she studies herself in*
m   *the mirror.*

e   It can be very difficult to be both honest and *sensitive* at the same time. These two qualities can sometimes seem completely at odds with each other. But they aren't. You simply have to think
n   creatively and couple any criticism with a compliment.

   You might first want to ask your friend if she or her mother picked out the dress. If it was her
t   mother, then you can relax and say something like, "Honestly, it's nice, but I don't think it's really you. Don't you think that pink outfit you picked out yourself last week looks better on you? You look great in it!" In this way you'll have subtly shifted the focus to how good *her* taste is.

   However, if she did pick out this dress, things get trickier. First, you might say, "It is nice, but, you know, I think it doesn't fit you as well as some other things you own." Point out places where it's too big or too small so she won't feel you're telling her she's too fat or skinny. If you think the pattern puts pounds on her, then say something like, "You know, those stripes are pretty, but I don't think they show off your figure." In this way you will be complimenting her by urging her to display something about herself that is very attractive. Finally, suggest that you go with her to return the dress and pick something else out. And when you do, be sure it's her day. Don't start trying on dresses also. *You* are not the focus here.

school or with other friends. But it's important to remember that it takes time to grow, learn, and change. Sometimes it can seem to take forever to work out a problem or change a bad habit or simply cheer up! Your friends need to know that you will give them the room they need to sort out their often confused feelings. You, after all, need the same from them.

noncompetitiveness

There is always something we admire about our friends. But sometimes, in particular when we are feeling insecure about ourselves, that admiration can turn into a feeling of competition or jealousy. This is not a very pleasant emotion and it can cause people to behave in equally unpleasant ways. Some people purposefully never compliment their friends. Others say mean things behind their back, and still others criticize friends just to make themselves feel better. No good! Chances are your friends have insecurities of their own. Think how bad they might feel! Remember, your friends admire things about you too. Spend your energies concentrating on your strengths, not theirs!

trust

Trust is *critical* in a friendship. Your friends need to know that you will be responsible enough to keep a secret or not repeat a sensitive comment to another person. They need to know you will take the time to understand their feelings about someone's teasing remark or a poor grade and not make fun of them. Most of all, they need to trust that they can be less than perfect and still be liked.

thoughtfulness

True friends think about each other even when they're not together. Remembering to bring a sick friend a treat, making a phone call to a friend you know is upset, and offering to help someone study for a test are all signs of thoughtfulness. Being good to a friend who asks for a favor is very nice. Letting your friend know he or she doesn't have to ask is even nicer.

honesty

Being *sensitive* but honest about what you think and who you are is the only way to be a good friend. True friendships exist only when you are being true to yourself. Otherwise you are simply lying to your friends. If you state an opinion about a problem your friend is having, he or she needs to know you really mean it. By having faith in your view, he or she can think more clearly about the problem. If what you feel remains unclear, your friend is not getting what he or she deserves most from your friendship—another way of looking at things, which can help him or her learn and grow.

Sometimes we have to give something up to help a friend. You might have to bypass a tennis game to help a friend who is temporarily on crutches get home safely from school. But it's a funny thing about sacrifice: The moment you give something up, you get something back. And that is the wonderful sense of having truly given. It sounds romantic, but I don't mean it that way. It simply feels very good to put your own needs aside to help someone else.

m i s e r a b l e

o
m
e
n
t

A friend bursts into your room, filled with excitement about a pre-camp get-together. "Can I borrow your new shirt?" she asks. "I want to look just right." Horrified, you reply, "Please don't ask me that! I haven't even worn it yet!" Suddenly her mood turns sour. "Great friend you are," she proclaims. "I'd lend you mine!"

Well, maybe she would and maybe she wouldn't. That is beside the point. No one can predict accurately 100 percent of the time how they would act if they were in another person's shoes. Besides, one could argue it's unfair of her to put you in this position!

So, putting aside any guilt you might feel over your reaction, what can you do? First, you can realize your friend is wildly worked up about this party and so the accusation that you are being less than a friend should be ignored. What she means is that she's upset you don't seem to realize how important this is to her. You need to show her you do "get it" but that you'd like to help her in another way. First, you might try explaining calmly that you were planning to wear your shirt to something special yourself and that you're afraid something could happen to it. Secondly, you could show her that you want to help by suggesting the two of you look to see what else in your wardrobe or hers could make a great outfit. But whatever you do, don't give in to keep the peace. That's not fair to either of you. Helping is not giving in. Helping is giving. And in this case you are offering your understanding, time, interest, and patience.

sharing

Good friends don't hoard their good fortune. If someone bakes you some delicious cookies, it is nice to share them. If a friend is going to a very special party and wants to borrow your necklace (as long as it's not incredibly expensive and you are allowed to lend it), it's nice to share that too. Sharing is a way of saying, "I want you to enjoy the nice things that happen to me." It's a very unselfish way to be and it allows your friends to see how much you'd like them to be happy. That can only inspire good feelings.

understanding

True understanding occurs in a friendship when one friend puts aside his or her own feelings in order to recognize what is going on for the other. If a good friend has just come in last in a swimming meet and snaps at you because he or she has lost a sneaker, it would be very understanding to just swallow your feelings and help look for the sneaker. Sure, later, when things are calmer, you could say, "I must say, you were turning purple after that race!" and see if you get an apology. But don't hold your breath. Friends have a right to know that small offenses will be forgiven without a word.

sensitivity

Friends try not to hurt each other. They know what each other's sore spots are, attempt to put themselves in the other's shoes, and always make an effort to be gentle during even the most difficult conversations. Friends also try not to blurt things out impulsively. If your friend has just come down with the flu right before a big party, he or she is probably not the one to whom you might excitedly exclaim, "I got the greatest new outfit for Saturday night!" When you keep your friends' feelings in mind before you act, you're using one of the five building blocks of social savvy.

reliability

Your friends need to know you can be counted on. If you make plans, stick to them. If you state an opinion, don't change it the next

o

m

e

n

t

A good friend keeps borrowing money and clothing from you, but you never see any of it again. Now she's asking you to lend her a dollar, which she will pay back "as soon as I get my allowance . . . promise!"

No matter what, you have every right to ask for the return of things you have lent. But how you handle this depends on the circumstances of your friend.

If this is someone who has a nice wardrobe and gets a regular generous allowance (and is therefore being quite irresponsible), then you might be very direct (with a bit of humor mixed in). "You know, I've loaned you so many things, and I haven't gotten anything back! Fair is fair! You owe me eight dollars and you still have my pink sweater, blue shorts, and striped socks! Please give me back my clothes and tell me when you can give me all the money. I can't loan you another dollar because you've already emptied my piggy bank!"

On the other hand, if this is someone from very modest circumstances, it could be she hasn't returned the sweater because she still needs it, and hasn't returned the money because it's taking her a while to save enough to pay you back. Of course, neither of these things is your fault. You are still entitled to the return of your belongings. But your approach to the subject would need to be gentle. Your friend is probably already quite embarrassed. "I really can't loan you any more money because, honestly, I'm on a budget too and you already owe me eight dollars. In fact, I was hoping to get at least some of it back from you soon. And that goes for my clothes too! I really wanted to wear my blue shorts this weekend." What you are doing here is offering her a payback schedule that she can handle. A little of the money and an item of clothing is a good start. It doesn't ask too much of her, but it does make it clear this can't go on indefinitely.

No matter what her circumstances, your friend is not going to be thrilled. But when someone borrows something, it is a particular kind of arrangement. It's not fair for the rules to change once the loan is made.

day. If you have borrowed something from a friend, return it in good shape and on time. This kind of behavior says, "I *respect* your time, your things, and, most important, you."

strength

Sometimes life can be quite difficult and painful. The parent of a friend might be very ill. Your friend may have had a bad accident and is stuck in the hospital. Or, a close buddy may be dreadfully upset over his parents' divorce. It isn't always easy to maintain friendships under these circumstances because staying friends means putting aside your own needs more often than usual and facing situations

m i s e r a b l e

m o m e n t

You notice that a very good friend of yours is starting to hang out with a wild crowd. In fact, you think you can already see some changes in the way he acts. You want to say something, but you're afraid he'll accuse you of sounding like his mother.

When people we care for start heading in a dangerous direction, we often feel that we ought to *do* something—as though if we made the right move, all would be well again. This isn't so. You can try to help, and in fact you should try. But the only person who can make the decision to change direction is your friend.

If your friend is traveling down a dangerous road, he might be quite defensive if you say anything negative. This is because deep in his heart he may have some doubts as well. The problem is, they may be doubts he doesn't want to listen to yet. If you want to be sure the two of you keep communicating, it may be best to phrase your thoughts in an interested, as opposed to accusatory, way. For instance, "Didn't Jimmy get picked up for shoplifting a couple of months ago? That would make me nervous" sounds better than "How can you hang out with someone who was caught shoplifting?" Or, "Doesn't Jill do a lot of drugs? She doesn't strike me as a very happy person" is better than "You know, if you keep hanging out with Jill, you might start doing drugs too."

The point is this: The best kind of help you can give is a way out. If your friend knows he can talk to you—if he feels that you're still his friend and that you support him—then he will have that much more strength to make important decisions. Let him know you are concerned about what he's doing. Be careful not to come on as if you were passing judgment or telling him what to do. That would make him stop listening altogether.

you'd rather not look at. It takes strength and *know-how* to stick by friends who are in trouble. But doing so often builds the strongest friendships of all.

compromise

No two friends always agree on what they want to do every time they get together. Nor can they agree about every issue that life throws their way. But what they can do, and in fact what they must do, is learn to bend, to *compromise*—another social savvy building block. Agreeing to see a movie with a star-struck friend when you're more in the mood for ice-skating may be a positive move. It expresses your willingness to allow for someone else's feelings. You aren't ignoring your own needs. You are simply making room for someone else's. And the *compromise?* Next weekend the two of you can sharpen your blades!

loyalty

Friends need to feel that they are there for each other. They need to sense that an argument or the attentions of a popular new person or an unfriendly rumor will not destroy the friendship. Loyalty means sticking by, and sticking up for, someone. More than anything else, it means allowing everyone to see that you place a very great value on your friendship with someone, and that it is not an easy thing to erase.

This last quality, loyalty, in fact, brings me to a very important issue, one which everyone contends with at one time or other—namely, the Great Popularity Myth. What do these two topics have to do with each other? Nothing. And that's just the point.

the great popularity myth

Popularity looks good. It may even feel good for a little while. But it isn't everything. In fact, it only means something if you are truly well liked. But popularity doesn't necessarily mean that at all. What it does

miserable

moment

It's the day of the big spelling test and you and your friend are on your way to school. "Boy," you comment, "I was up real late last night studying for this test. But I think I know most of it." "Oh, good!" your friend exclaims. "Can I peek just a little at your paper during the test? I'm terrible at spelling."

You are in a very difficult position. You have a friend in need and you want to help. Unfortunately, his idea of "help" doesn't feel good. Cheating is not only unfair to you, considering the amount of work you put in, but also to your friend. If he cheats, he will have learned nothing and more than likely need to keep cheating just to keep up. So what do you do? First of all, take *responsibility* for your beliefs and tell your friend you just wouldn't feel comfortable allowing him to cheat. Explain why, making sure to include the point that if he were caught, you would get in trouble too. (It's important to remind him that if you allowed him to cheat, both of you would be doing some-thing wrong.) Then offer a *compromise*. Offer, for instance, to give up your lunch hour to help him study his spelling. Assure him it would help a lot, and let him know you have a few spelling tricks you'd be happy to pass on. In other words, make it clear that you *do* want to help. It's just that you want to find a way that will work for both of you. Helping him *earn* his good grade is a very savvy goal. It also proves that you are a tremendously good friend.

mean is that the popular person is admired, often imitated, and certainly granted a lot of power to decide what's "cool," what's fun, and who's okay.

The most savvy thing to realize about popularity is that it can be given and it can be taken away. You cannot own it. Whether or not a person is popular depends on the needs, desires, whims, and opinions of others.

What a shaky boat that is!

Wouldn't you rather be out at sea with a boat that *you* can steer, instead of being bounced around by any wave that comes along? Well, the only way to do that is to like yourself, be yourself, and be good to your friends.

The minute you put more faith in yourself than in the opinions of

60 •

social savvy

others, you will be a lot stronger and happier. Being "popular" because you're a kind, considerate person who is fun to be with is a wonderful thing—because if your popularity should ebb, you will still have a few good friends by your side.

the savvy balancing act

Most people have more than one friend. This is good because everyone has lots of different needs and not all of them can be met by only one person. One friend might be especially helpful with school problems, another might be better at talking over family troubles, and still another might be great fun on camping trips. Also, since not every friend will need you at the same moment, you can usually be there when the need arises.

However, life being the way it is, often things are not so simple. Two friends may want to see you on the same afternoon. You may be desperate to talk to someone who already has other plans. Two out of three of you might be in a terrible fight, and each may want you to take sides. Things can get awfully tricky when people care about each other but have very different needs at the same moment.

Here is a survival guide to help you "balance," with a lot of savvy, the good friends you'd like to keep!

One friend asks to make a date the same day you have one with another friend.

Simply say you're sorry but you've already made plans. Then, so it's clear you are not rejecting him or her, add something like, "Why don't we make plans right now for getting together on Monday or Tuesday?"

Your friend wants to know whom you are going to be with and if she could join you.

m i s e r a b l e

m

o

m

e

n

t

An acquaintance, somebody you sit next to in your painting class, keeps asking you to do something with him over the weekend. You enjoy talking with him as you paint, but you're really not interested in spending any time with him other than that.

You do not have to be friends with everyone you know. But you do still have to accord them respect and sensitivity. Acquaintances are people you may talk with very casually and whom you know only on a surface level. This is allowed. That's why the word is in the dictionary! However, it can get sticky if one person decides he would like to be more than just an acquaintance while the other has no desire for change.

The kindest, and therefore most savvy, way to handle this predicament is to turn him down repeatedly with vague but truthful excuses such as, "I have too much schoolwork" or "I'm sorry, but I already have other plans." Offered often enough, your acquaintance will stop asking without "losing face." However, be prepared. He may also seem less willing to simply chat with you, because his feelings might be hurt. If he steps away, you'll have to let him. It would be nice if we could have everything just the way we wanted it. But we can't. Not when it comes to dictating how other people feel or behave. That's up to them.

If there's no reason not to tell your friend whom you will be with, then go ahead. But if you would like this particular date to be a two-some, be firm but positive. "I don't think that's a great idea this time. But maybe we could all go to the movies next weekend" would be just fine. It lets her know that even though you'd like to spend some time on your own with someone else, you have no intention of excluding her on a regular basis.

You've already made plans with one friend, but another calls and is very upset about a problem. He asks if you can break your date to see him.

This is a hard one. Generally speaking, it's not nice to break a date with anyone. But there are exceptions. First, however, you might immediately try to draw your friend out. "Tell me what's got you so upset. Maybe we could talk about it now" would make it clear that you do care. If the problem doesn't seem too bad, you might say that you can't break the date but you'd be happy to get together first thing the next day or after school. However, if it is a painful problem, you might want to consider breaking the date (making sure to apologize to your other friend and set up a rain date). A friend in serious need shouldn't be ignored. But do explain to your friend with whom you are breaking the date that it's not a whim—you have to help someone.

You would like to see a friend who has just told you she's busy. You think to yourself, "Why didn't she make a date with me?"

As I said earlier, every friendship is slightly different because each person offers something different in a friendship. Perhaps this friend is easy to play tennis with because she plays for fun—not to win, like you. Maybe she understands another friend's personal problem better than most—or, yes, better than you. These facts don't make her better than you, or even a more desirable friend to others. What they do make her is the right choice of a friend to other people as well as you, at particular times. You can live with that, can't you?

Two friends are in a terrible argument and each wants you to side with him. You can see both sides and would rather stay out of it.

Good idea! But don't take it too far. There is often a middle ground. It's called *mediating*. That means to take an objective position and help each side listen, understand, and reach a solution or *compromise*. It would be very savvy to explain to both of your friends that you don't want to take sides because you care about them both and the argument has nothing to do with you. However, you wouldn't mind being there with them to help them reach a middle ground. In offering to be involved in this way, not only will you be showing that you are a concerned friend, but you will also be giving each person the sense that something can be worked out.

balancing friends and parents

Probably, your parents will approve of most of your friends. If you like someone, chances are they will see why. But still, there may be a few friends who will not meet with your parents' approval. Perhaps they think this friend is impolite. Maybe they fear one friend is too wild and could get you in trouble. Then again, perhaps they've heard something about a friend's family that makes them uncomfortable and they would rather you not visit there.

Whatever the problem, parental disapproval of a friend can hurt both you and your friend very much. Your parents might be quite right to feel concerned, or they may not. Whatever the truth, it would be wise to keep your savvy building blocks in mind and to patiently hear what your parents have to say. The simple act of your listening will help your parents feel that you *respect* them and want to make thoughtful decisions. It will help them trust your opinions and sense of *responsibility* all the more. If they're wrong, you will be better able to answer their concerns. If they're right, you will have learned something important about your friend before any serious trouble could erupt.

Here's a guide to the most common dilemmas between young people, their parents, and their friends.

Your parents feel your friend is very rude.

Well, is she? Watch what happens when she walks in the door. Does she head straight for your room without even nodding at your father? Does she go into the kitchen and open up the refrigerator with barely a smile at your parents? If it appears to you that she is indeed a little rude, don't deny it to your parents. Instead, let them know you will try to fix the problem. Then, when you and your friend can talk

social savvy

quietly, casually say something like, "You know, I notice when you walk in my house, you act like my parents aren't even there! I have a feeling it bothers them. Try to remember to say 'Hi' and ask them how they are, okay?" Be sure not to sound as if you are accusing her of something awful. Sometimes friends don't acknowledge parents because they are uncomfortable with adults. Other times it may be because they simply were not taught good manners. So be both direct and *sensitive*. Chances are things will improve.

Your parents think that your friend is too wild and that he's going to get you in trouble.

Is he? Sometimes a friend just appears to be wild. He may like to dress in a daring way and put on airs, while in truth he may be more conservative than you! If this is true of your friend, explain this to your parents and be sure to give examples. However, if your friend *is* a little devil-may-care, it's possible your parents may have a point. Tell them so, and let them know you will *compromise* in the way you handle the friendship. Avoiding your friend altogether may not be the solution, but keeping away in certain circumstances may be ideal. If, for instance, your friend often behaves in an unruly fashion at the movies, you may want to avoid seeing films with him. If your parents see you are treating their views with *respect* and maturity, they will more than likely feel reasonably comfortable, allowing you to keep this friend.

Your parents have put their foot down. They feel a particular friend is a bad influence and they do not want you seeing her.

Do they have reason to feel this strongly about your friend? Give it careful thought. Perhaps your grades have been slipping. Maybe you have been a bit too rowdy after school and the teachers were right to complain. This may not mean that you have to completely end the friendship forevermore. But it does mean you should probably take some time to responsibly own up to the truth and honor your parents' request. Certainly, you will still be able to chat with your friend at school, but it may be time to direct your attention toward yourself! First, without placing blame on your parents, explain to your friend why you can't spend any extra time together. After all, she didn't *make* you do anything. Clearly, you wanted to behave as you did for your own reasons. After a cooling-off period, in which you have taken the time to work harder and find other outlets for your need to "let go" (such as jogging, art, dance), you might approach your parents. "Look. I did what you said. I understand why you felt the way you did. But I think it has given my friend and me time to think about what we've been doing and me a chance to see things more clearly. Can I invite her over here so you can see for yourself that I can handle things better?" In this way you will be making it clear that you have no interest in sneaking any relationships by them. This in turn will make them trust you and your judgments more. They may still say no, but with a little more time they might soften—especially as the evidence builds that you've taken *responsibility* for your life.

Your friend's family has a well-known history of problems and your parents don't want you going over there.

Depending on the problem, this is a tough one. If, for instance, your friend's parent is an alcoholic, unexpected trouble could erupt in the household that neither you nor your friend should have to handle. In this case you might want to go along with your parents' judgment. Or, perhaps it's your friend's older brother who is rumored to be involved with drugs. Your parents may view this as too much of a temptation for you or simply too dangerous. If there are drugs and older kids in the house, trouble could brew. However, if there are less serious problems, such as lots of unpleasant arguing in the household or unemployment problems, you and your parents might have room to talk. Their chief concern is that you won't be drawn into or upset by any difficult aspect of your friend's household. If you can convince them

that what they've heard does not make it difficult for you to visit—
"When her parents start yelling, we go down to the basement and turn
on loud music. Besides, I think she needs me"—then chances are
they'll allow you to go occasionally! (Pay attention, however, to
whether your friend is comfortable having visitors. Sometimes people
with difficult home lives would rather do the visiting instead of being
visited.)

Your parents need to know you are listening to them. They only
want to protect you from hurt, and sometimes they do know more than
you. Then again, there will be times when it is you who sees things
most clearly. After all, what your parents see is often colored by their
fears for you. In the end, it's critical that you and your parents talk
openly. That way all of you can learn from one another.

tempering expectations

There are few things that will ruin a friendship faster than unreal-
istic expectations. I have already said that different friends are capable of different things. No one friend can offer you everything you
need. But sometimes we feel so close to someone that we forget they
are only human. We expect and expect and expect until suddenly we
find ourselves up against a brick wall—and it hurts. Perhaps you've
been studying for the lead role in the school play and your friend has
been doing a great job of soothing your nerves. Every night he or she
has calmed you down. But now, two nights before the first perfor-
mance, you've just called your friend and he or she has company and
can't talk. You feel disappointed and then angry. But your friend, who
has been there for you in so many ways, is horrified that you can forget
all your friend has done just because he or she was unavailable this
once. The two of you can barely speak.

Keep in mind that just as you cannot be everything for your friend,
your friend cannot be everything for you. What counts is the whole
picture. Does your friend usually understand you? Is your friend loyal

to you and sensitive to your needs? If the answer is yes, then perhaps it's up to you to back off a bit. If you have need of some comfort or companionship, call another friend.

weathering the bad times

There is no friendship in the world that runs smoothly all the time. Everyone is different and no matter how much you have in common with someone else, you are bound to have rough times. Rather than indicating a relationship is in trouble, as most people think, moments of conflict often mean that a friendship is ticking along well—that people are being honest with each other and facing their feelings. Sometimes you may feel misunderstood, other times very hurt, and still other times angry and frustrated. We've already explored how to

m i s e r a b l e

m o m e n t

Something you've said in anger about your friend to someone else is repeated to her. Now she is confronting you. "How could you have said that about me?" she practically screams. "I thought you were my friend!"

Your first temptation may be to deny the whole thing. Don't do it. She knows the truth, and asking her to believe otherwise would only make her feel even more distrustful of you than she already is.

Acknowledge you said it, explaining you were very angry when you blurted out the words. Then apologize for hurting her and move on to express why you said it at all. Speak truthfully but carefully. "Of course I didn't mean it when I said you *always* brag about how well you do in school. But I didn't feel good when you kept talking about your A in math when I only got a C+" is a good example. It makes it clear you were exaggerating because you were hurt. This will make the whole unfortunate circumstance a little easier to understand and thus easier to forget. It will ring true because it is true. Your friend will be able to regain some faith in you, and both you and she will have learned when to keep both of your mouths closed.

express anger in Chapter Two. But now let's take a look at what to do (and not to do) when a friendship is threatening to move from being warm and fun to distant and upsetting.

the wrong moves

Very often when people become upset with each other, it feels safer to express those difficult feelings indirectly—not up front and in the open. But it isn't safer. In fact, it's much more dangerous to a friendship than a frank, angry confrontation could ever be. All that being "indirect" accomplishes is confusion. And all confusion accomplishes is the unraveling of a friendship. Here are some guidelines for those touchy situations.

> ### class quote
> The group was deep in discussion about friendship when one person raised her hand and said, "When I get angry at my best friend, I don't think I like her anymore." Everyone in the group nodded—including me. "I know just what you mean," I replied. "But I notice when my friend and I talk things through, I'm not angry anymore. A friendship can sometimes travel down a bumpy road. It may be hard, but stay with it. When the road clears, things are often smoother than ever!"

• *Don't* ignore each other. Some people like to let you know they're angry by giving you the cold shoulder. This unfortunately paves the way for lots of confusion and *no* resolution of the problem. If you're not speaking, how can you work out the problem?

• *Don't* say hurtful things. Some people would rather say spiteful things that have nothing to do with what they're angry about than face the true issue. This way they can be sure to hurt their friend (which they think will make them feel better, but it never does) without having to face a trying conversation. This action is particularly bad because even if the two friends are finally able to sort out the real problem, it's hard to forget when a good friend betrays your trust by picking at your sensitive spot.

• *Don't* make a new "best friend" too fast. Some people, once they've been hurt, would rather just run away than face the problem. Finding another "better" friend seems the easiest thing to do. But this never works. First of all, the choice of a new friend is usually made in such haste that it's often not the right match in the long run. And secondly, that original friendship deserves so much more than a hasty retreat! The very fact that there is any hurt at all indicates there is real caring. Running from one person to the next will only leave a trail of unanswered questions and unresolved problems. It certainly won't lead to new friendships—because being friends means sticking together through the rough times.

m i s e r a b l e

m o m e n t

You are playing cards with a friend who is losing. Suddenly in midstream he begins changing the rules, insisting these are what they've always been. You are getting very angry but don't want to cause so big an argument that you lose a friend.

It would be a good idea to excuse yourself and go to the kitchen for something cool to drink. Very angry feelings rarely result in good problem-solving. Most people when confronted with someone else's anger will simply react defensively. They will spend all their time sticking up for themselves instead of looking at where they might be at fault—which is, of course, a very important aspect of resolving an argument.

When you come back into the room, hopefully feeling more relaxed, you might say something like, "Look. Now you've got me confused. Just to refresh both of our memories, let's go over the rules." When he gets to the part you disagree with, point out how, had this been so, then earlier in the game you would have accumulated more points. This will give him pause. The two of you could either stop the current game, call it a draw, and begin again, or honor the original rules. In either case, it would be a good idea to write down the rules *before* you begin to play.

The next time you feel hurt, disappointed, or angry in a friendship, face the feelings. But first, and this is critical, *do so alone*. When difficult emotions first surface, they have a way of coloring everything. They can make you forget what's good about your friendship. If you talk to your friend before you are truly ready, a lot of unfair and untrue things could be said. Much of it might never be forgotten and could break the trust you've shared even if you do resume the friendship. It's important to take the time to allow your feelings to subside and remind yourself of the good things. I suggest the following two-part plan:

1. Write your friend a letter, but don't let him or her see it.

    You are entitled to unfair feelings, tremendously angry thoughts, and bitter reactions. The trouble is, they could destroy a good friendship if they were presented just the way you feel them without regard for all the facts or your friend's feelings. So, write them down! Tell your friend in a letter all of the awful things you'd like to say. "I never met anyone more selfish!" or "You are without a doubt the most insensitive person I've ever met!" Keep writing until you've gotten it all out! You'll be surprised at how much better you feel.

2. List the things that are good about both your friend and your relationship.

    Now that you feel a little calmer, it's important to look at the whole picture. By remembering what has made the friendship so strong and the qualities your friend possesses that you benefit from and admire, you will feel a little less cheated, hurt, or angry. That in turn will help you decide more carefully what you will say when you both speak, and will naturally result in a much more positive conversation.

No one likes to feel that they are "all bad" or "all wrong." And that's only fair. After all, few people are! If you take the time to look at the situation fairly, it will be easier to work the problem out with honesty and *sensitivity*.

calling a friendship quits

Sometimes a friendship just doesn't work. You try, but somehow both of you just keep disappointing each other. You would like to end the friendship, but you don't know how. So you keep making dates, all the while feeling bored, upset, or uncomfortable. There is no one way to ease out of a relationship. You have a few options.

• You could say something like, "Lately I have been feeling that we're not getting along that well. Maybe we should back off a little right now." This is the most direct way to handle the problem and it leaves the door open for a later time when the two of you might be friends again.
• You might just quietly and indirectly let things drift. When your friend calls to make plans, politely say you're already busy; or if he or she suggests getting together at some future date, say you think you might be busy then and so you can't make plans. He or she will know what you are doing and may or may not press the issue. If your friend doesn't pursue it, you will know that he or she, like yourself, is also more comfortable with an indirect approach to at least a temporary good-bye. If your friend does question you, you will have to be straight with him or her.
• If you're upset, and that's why you need to step away, then say so. "I'm just too upset to make plans with you right now. I need to take some time off from our friendship." Again, you may want to be friends in the future. Handling your feelings this way gives you both time and space. And that is just what you need to decide if the friendship could work at a later date.

One final note on ending friendships. It can feel overwhelmingly sad to say good-bye to someone you've been close to. This is because you've shared and cared a lot. But this is something you will face throughout your life. People change. What makes a good friend at one point in time does not necessarily hold true later on. What's important is that we treat the friends we have with the *respect* and *sensitivity* they deserve—from start to finish.

It isn't always easy. It takes *know-how*. But in doing so, we become the kind of friends we would like to have in others. And that is the basis for true friendship savvy.

2

savvy

every

day,

everywhere

FOUR

table settings are just the beginning

*W*hen it comes to an enjoyable meal, tasty food is certainly important. I myself have shelves and shelves of cookbooks that I always refer to when planning what I hope will be a delicious feast. But no matter how carefully I follow the recipe—adding a quarter of a teaspoon of oregano, a dash of lemon juice, a third of a cup of cooking sherry—I remain well aware that a good dining experience is not solely dependent on good food. What do I mean?

When it comes to a great meal, delicious food can truly be appreciated only if the setting is attractive, if everyone seated is being considerate of one another, and if each person feels comfortable and confident at the table. In other words, a scrumptious dish of spaghetti and meatballs served at a dirty table to people who are inhaling their pasta from a fork held six inches above their face is simply not going to taste as good as the same dish served at a well-laid-out table to people who are twirling the spaghetti neatly with a fork, dropping every bit into their mouth—and nowhere else!

There is a reason for this. When we eat, we are using all five of our senses. If any one of them is offended, it takes away from the mealtime experience. We use our sight to admire the pretty colors and shapes of both the food and the table setting. What we see inspires us to happily anticipate the food. Our sense of smell takes in the lovely aromas that serve to whet our appetite. Our ears allow us to enjoy warm conversation and to listen to the delicate sounds of forks touching plates and cups being placed in saucers. We use our sense of touch when we pick up a cool glass of water or tear a piece of bread and are thus reminded we are about to have a satisfying experience.

And, of course, there is our sense of taste, which allows us to appreciate the delicious flavors that distinguish one food from another.

All of our senses come together to add or subtract from our mealtime enjoyment, and so it is important that we consider every aspect of the dining experience. Cookbooks alone simply cannot ensure a fabulous meal. Only you and those around you can do that.

creating the table

There is nothing like an attractive table to make your guests feel welcome and, well, *hungry!* A light-blue color scheme chosen because it's one of your guest's favorite shades, or a delightful centerpiece of fall leaves and bright-red apples to top off a day of hiking, or even just a single wildflower in a tiny vase at each place setting all say the same thing: "Sitting down to eat together is an important and wonderful experience." Of course, delicious aromas floating in from the kitchen are also inviting, but the meal begins when people take their seat and look at what is before them. It should be as well planned as the menu.

table-setting know-how

There are some people who believe that as long as everything is clean and neat it doesn't really matter where you place your dishes and utensils. I am not one of them. I think it's always important to lay your table out the correct way. This is so for two reasons. To begin with, the proper way actually makes sense. For example, the salad fork—because it is used first—should be on the outside. Secondly, there's something to be said for elegance and tradition. Sticking to "rules," as I explained earlier in this book, does not mean you are old-fashioned or weird, but rather that you care. It's that simple. So here are the basics.

silverware

A well-set table might have as few as three pieces of silverware at a setting, or as many as six or more. It all depends on the spirit of the meal, the occasion, the food, and the time of day. The simpler the setting, the more informal the meal. But no matter how you choose to serve, the rules remain the same: Placement is according to use. Each person begins with the outside utensils and works his or her way in.

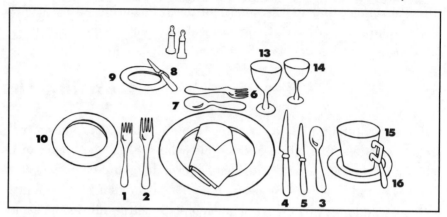

Above is a simple illustration for a full dinner. Notice the order in which everything is placed. The salad fork (1) is placed on the outside left because it will be used before the dinner fork (2). The soup spoon (3) is placed on the outside right of the knives, since it will be used before the knives. The dinner knife (4) lies directly beside the dinner plate with the blade facing inward. The salad knife (5) lies to the right of the dinner knife. Some people place both a dessert fork (6) and spoon (7) above their dinner plates. You may use them together, "European style," to eat cakes or pastries. The spoon is used in place of a knife. Sometimes, a butter knife (8) may also be included in the setting, resting across the bread and butter dish (9).

• savvy tips

• If you are serving a quick meal, it is quite all right simply to set a fork, knife, and dessert spoon as described above.
• There is only one fork that is allowed on the right of the dinner knife and it is a rather odd-looking seafood, or lobster, fork. (See page 97 for an illustration.)
• Remember, if you are using plastic utensils, keep a few extra on hand. They often break.

Depending on the way you are serving, the dinner table setting may include, as mentioned, the smaller bread and butter plate (9) and the slightly larger salad or vegetable plate (10), both of which are placed to the left of the dinner plate, or entrée (pronounced "on-tray") plate, as it is sometimes called. Many people, if they are electing to eat their salad course before the main meal, will set their table with the salad plate sitting on the dinner plate. You can also serve the salad "European style": Here the salad, with a light vinaigrette dressing, is served after the main course and before dessert, to "cleanse the palate"— the idea being garlic and chocolate soufflé don't mix! The soup bowl should always be served upon a plate, both of which should be removed when the course is finished.

• savvy tips

• Salad plates often double as dessert plates, so if you have only a limited number as most people do, be sure to wash them quickly in between courses so they'll be ready for some delicious treats!
• Soup bowls come in two shapes. Consommé (11), which usually has a delicate handle on either side, and a shallow bowl with a rim (12), which looks much like the dinner plate. Generally, as the names indicate, light cream soups, thin broths, or consommés are served in the former, while thicker, chunkier soups are served in the latter.

a word about place setting and serving

I occasionally refer to the placement and use of silverware on a plate in terms of telling time on a clock. The handles of the utensils are the arms and the plate is the face. Trust me. It makes things very clear!

Also, I occasionally refer to the European style of doing things. This doesn't mean you should wait for a trip to Paris before giving it a try. It's simply another way of serving and eating with which you should be familiar, and which is perfectly acceptable this side of the Atlantic.

glassware

Usually a single glass is placed at the top right of your place setting. On fancier occasions, a water goblet (13) and a wine glass (14) may be placed to the right of the plate instead.

• savvy tips

• The coffee cups and saucers (15) come out with dessert and are placed to the right of the dessert dish. You can place your coffee- or teaspoon (16) on the rim of the saucer.
• Never use very tall, slender drinking glasses unless you are serving iced tea or lemonade, which is traditionally served slim and cold and just about always with a straw!

napkins

The only rule that governs the placement of dinner napkins on the table is: Keep them neat and attractive. They can sit in any number of places: to the left of the dinner plates with the forks resting either on top or alongside, blossoming out of the water goblets as if they were flowers, folded neatly and resting flat in the center of the dinner plates, or shaped in any number of artistic ways and, again, set in the center of the dinner plates

Here are some creative examples of napkin folding that may bring out the artist in you.

• savvy tips

• Cocktail napkins, which may be used as coasters or to hold small appetizers when one is not sitting at the dinner table, are usually made of linen or decorative paper. They are quite small, as they are intended only to catch a few crumbs and protect furniture against water stains. Theirs is a small but important job, so don't forget to put them out!
• Tablecloths or place mats should always be clean and pressed. I prefer tablecloths when there are many people sitting at the table, because place mats with their clearly defined lines seem to add clutter

o

m

e

n

t

The person sitting next to you at a wedding reception has started to drink out of your glass. You're very thirsty and now you have no glass.

The reason someone might make this mistake is because he or she is either not think- ing, or unaware that the glass is always set on the right. Glass placement, however, is not an earth-shattering piece of information and thus it is certainly not worth embarrassing anyone. When a waiter passes by, ask for a glass of water. If you cannot find a waiter, simply smile at your neighbor nicely and say, "Hmm. I think you've got my glass. Might I have yours?" and nod toward the empty one to his or her right.

to a table already laden with utensils and plates. The variety of table-cloths is endless, whether it be an embroidered one, or perhaps one that is hand-crocheted with a solid-color cloth underneath, with napkins to match. Perhaps, as an alternative, a very pretty floral sheet! And let us not forget another option: a paper or plastic tablecloth. Needless to say, the paper is disposable and the plastic can be just wiped clean! However, when I'm serving a dinner for four to six people, I often use place mats to create different moods, though my dishes remain the same. (Red-and-white-checked mats with white plates look very different in spirit from lace-edged white mats with the same dishes.)

buffet tables

People will often elect to serve buffet style when there a lot of guests coming and there is not enough room to seat everyone around the dining room table. There are two ways to serve buffet. I call them "Whole note" (for the full buffet) and "Half note" (for the semi-buffet).

At a "Whole note" buffet, guests serve themselves in the dining room or kitchen and then sit down and hold their plate on their laps, setting their glass on the nearest table with a coaster or a cocktail napkin underneath.

At a "Half note" buffet, guests serve themselves in the dining room or kitchen and then sit down at any number of small tables, where places have already been set with silverware and glassware.

Generally, the plates, silverware, napkins, and main dish at a "Whole note" buffet are at the end of the table in front of the food presentation. The plates are usually piled one on top of another, but there are many ways to arrange everything else—for example, silverware in separate piles with the napkins folded and arranged in a fan shape, or a knife and fork wrapped up in each napkin, which might then be placed in a straw or silver basket. Mustard and other condiments rest on the opposite end of the table. Beverage glasses, if they are not at the place settings, are on a separate smaller table convenient to the buffet table. Any buffet table should be nicely decorated with, for example, a pretty tablecloth, candlesticks, and/or a large decorative piece in the center. A festive table piled high with good-looking food is an unbeatable way to say "Welcome!"

centerpieces and other forms of decoration

Centerpieces are a chance for you to be creative, festive, and thoughtful. There are really only two rules about centerpieces.

1. They should never overwhelm the rest of your table, attracting all the attention, instead of adding and completing the overall look. They should not touch in any way the utensils or dishes.
2. They should never be so large as to make it impossible for people to have a clear view of those sitting across the table. (If it feels as if you need to pass notes to your neighbor across the table, it's a safe bet the centerpiece is a bit too much.)

Now, apart from these two rules, you only need to keep the following point in mind: Centerpieces that work are those that catch the eye, express a feeling, reflect the occasion, or simply make people smile. As you can see, that opens up a lot of options. You can design traditional centerpieces using such things as flowers, candlesticks, autumn leaves, fresh fruit, or small potted plants. You can also be totally original using a collection of porcelain figurines, clear water-filled bowls with flower petals floating on top, or even a Mexican sombrero (if you're serving an "across the border" meal)!

Just to loosen you up a bit, here are a few more examples of perfectly wonderful centerpieces that can add a lot to your well-set table.

• A glass bowl filled with brightly colored candy canes and penny charms for the holiday season. (After the meal you can distribute its contents to your guests to munch on after dessert!)
• A straw basket filled with pastel-colored eggs on a bed of grass for Easter.
• An arrangement of small framed snapshots of you and your friends to celebrate the end of school year and the start of summer jobs or camp. (A touch of confetti strewn around the photos is a nice touch!)
• A goldfish bowl! (Make sure the water and bowl are clean and the fish have been fed in advance. Otherwise, you could create a mess.)
• A basket of unused tennis balls with a banner in the middle standing tall to celebrate a big win!
• A collection of beautiful seashells either strewn onto the center of the table or in a glass bowl is perfect for a seafood dinner.

some more savvy tips for a beautiful table

There are more decorative touches that can also contribute a great deal to the look.

• Napkins and tablecloths should either match or blend to create a pleasing look. A soft blue tablecloth with soft blue napkins can look as lovely as a white tablecloth with flowered napkins all around (as long as the plates aren't so busy that the table ends up looking like a four-ring circus—or ten—depending on how many people you have)!
• If you are throwing an exceptionally big dinner party and you do not have enough "good" dishes to go around, there are two good choices. Your first choice is to supplement what you do have with a package of good, solid, "designer" plastic dinner dishes color-coordinated with

the dishes you already own. Be sure to alternate around the table between the good china and the plastic dishes so that it will look like a decorative choice. (If you were to simply place three plastic dishes in a row at the point at which you ran out of china, it would look terribly obvious and leave three people feeling a bit insulted.) Your second choice is to just go out and purchase enough of those nice plastic dishes for everyone!

• Place cards are sometimes used when a lot of people will be dining together. Do make sure to spell everyone's name correctly and to do so in good penmanship. Place cards are usually not necessary with smaller parties and in fact one person I know has come up with a novel idea that serves much the same purpose. She purchases a trinket (costing no more than $1) for each guest that is a symbol of something special about him or her. She places each item where she would like each person to sit and then invites her guests to guess where they are meant to dine. For example, if a friend is driving across the country with her family for the summer, a small car-shaped eraser would be perfect! Another example is a set of mini-paints, or a mini-paintbrush, for a friend who loves to paint.

---

class quote

While I was demonstrating the proper way to set a table, one young man called out, "But what about when we eat with paper or plastic plates?" "Well," I answered, "let's see." I paused for effect. "Do you put your food on the paper plates?" He nodded. "And do you spear and cut your food with the plastic utensils?" He nodded again. "And are all these things arranged on a table?" Once again his head bobbed up and down. "Well," I concluded, "whether it's paper or fine china, it's still mealtime and still the same setup. Oh, and good luck. Sometimes plastic breaks. If that happens, just toss it, and grab another!"

One final note before we move on: Dining with paper plates and forks or eating in the kitchen or even sitting on a picnic blanket is no excuse for a lack of table manners! A messy, disorganized kitchen table will take away from the meal. A soiled picnic blanket coupled with napkins that aren't firm or plentiful enough to contend with greasy fried chicken could take away a lot of appetites. And broken plastic utensils can be terribly unpleasant to use, no matter how casual the situation. (Remember, always bring extra.)

basic table manners

From the moment you approach the dinner table till the moment you push back your chair at the end of the meal, it is important to keep in mind some basic table manners. Again, this has nothing to do with old Aunt Roberta or blindly following rules. It has to do with being RESPECTFUL and appreciative toward others, and showing that you know how to conduct yourself in a well-informed, savvy manner.

taking your seat

• You should always wait for the host or hostess to take his or her seat before you take yours. If your friend has organized the dinner, then he or she is the host. If you were invited to your friend's house for dinner with his or her family, then usually his or her mother would be considered the hostess.

• If you are a boy, it's nice to help the girl at your right into her seat by gently pulling out the chair and, when she is half-seated, pushing it in under her. Of course if the young lady on your left has no one to assist her, do step in. Then you can rest. No need to help everyone at the table!

• If you do not like where you are seated, sorry, but you'll have to live with it. It is extremely impolite to rearrange what your host has planned, and since it's likely that a guest or two will catch you in the act, feelings are bound to be hurt.

napkin etiquette

• The Ré Way, as I like to put it, is to place the napkin on your lap as soon as you sit down. However, if you are a guest at someone's table, then wait for your host or hostess to make the move before you do.

• When you leave the table during the meal for any reason, you should always put your napkin on your chair.

• When you wipe your mouth, use only a portion of the napkin, always bringing it up to your mouth, not the other way around. Dab your mouth on one side, then the middle, then the other side, and then replace it onto your lap. Never scrub. There's plenty of time for a bath later.

• Do not cough or sneeze into your napkin. Your napkin is intended to wipe your mouth. Need I say more?

• Do not tie your napkin around your neck or tuck it into your pants. Even if the colors look splendid together, you and the napkin will not!

m i s e r a b l e

o
m
e
n
t

You are at a crowded table, about to sneeze, and your mouth is full.

First try to finish what is in your mouth. If there's not enough time, turn your head toward your armpit and bring your hand up to your nose. Hopefully, you will have a handkerchief or tissue with you (never use your napkin). Keep your hand up at all times. People want to eat—not take a shower!

I know the above must seem like a lot to remember. But so much of it is just common sense. Take a moment to think about it and you'll see how much will stay with you. And besides, consider the benefits. Wouldn't it be nice to get through an entire dinner without your parents even once correcting your manners!

social savvy

• Food is served from the left and taken away from the right.

• If your host or hostess passes around a tray bearing sliced meat and some serving utensils, take the tray, help yourself to a modest portion, and replace the utensils onto the serving tray at the four-thirty position. Even if you're starving, it's important to make sure everyone has enough to eat. So *compromise,* and don't load your plate! Seconds are acceptable.

• When you are through serving yourself, always say "Thank you."

• Sometimes serving is done family style. This means the food is placed in the middle of the table and passed around by everyone seated. Here, too, it's important to take a modest amount unless you can see there is plenty to go around.

• If there is something on the table that you want, whether it's the salt shaker or the bowl of yams, simply say "Please pass the . . ." or "May I please have the . . ." Even if the item you are requesting is within arm's reach, if it would require you reaching across someone else's place setting, then don't do it. That is their space—not yours.

• There is nothing wrong with asking for seconds as long as you can see there is plenty left. Simply say something like, "This roast beef is delicious. May I please have a bit more?" Then pass your plate with your knife and fork at four o'clock balanced on the top. Used utensils should never be placed on the table. They make a terrible mess.

m i s e r a b l e   o m e n t

Your mouth is filled with food and someone asks you a question

Simply put one finger up in the air and continue to chew your food carefully. This person will see you need a moment and wait patiently for your answer. (There is an added benefit to this situation. It gives you time to think of a good answer!)

table talk

Good dinner-table conversation involves everyone at the table, and avoids subjects that could ruin one's appetite, offend someone, or depress everyone. There are of course so many subjects that are safe to bring up to a group of friends that I think it might be easier to give you a quick rundown of the don'ts.

• *Don't* tell dirty or gross jokes. Lots of people don't think they're funny.
• *Don't* tell tragic stories. It's upsetting to hear sad stories.
• *Don't* make racist comments. These aren't nice at anytime.
• *Don't* talk about your physical ailments. Guests could lose their appetite.
• *Don't* give descriptions of anything gory or bloody. Ditto!
• *Don't* discuss highly personal subjects. Remember, people don't like to be drawn in too close too fast. There's bound to be someone at your table who would feel uncomfortable.
• *Don't* gossip. You never know who at the table will be hurt, or where else the info might go. Passing it on is not your duty.
• *Don't* discuss topics that are of interest to only a few. It's rude to bring up a subject that only a few people at the table can discuss. The others will feel terribly left out. But if by accident this happens, give the others a little background on the situation. That way they can at least understand what is being said.

finishing up

• Contrary to popular opinion, there is no reason to leave some food on your plate. This practice was born of the belief that to finish every morsel indicates you really have not had enough to eat. I think that's silly. If you're hungry, eat whatever is on your plate. But, try not to take seconds that prove your eyes are bigger than your stomach, and whatever you do, don't scrape your fork across your plate searching for that last great flavorful taste. It will make you look like a bottom-less pit!
• When you have finished your meal, the fork and knife should be

social savvy

placed in the middle of the plate with the handles pointing to four-thirty or five-thirty. The knife blade should be facing you. (Do remember the fork comes first, just as in the alphabet.)

• Place your napkin on the table to the right of your plate. Folding it is unnecessary, but a crumpled or bunched-up look isn't right either. Just lay it down gently in a vertical shape.

• The table should be cleared completely before dessert. Nothing should be left but the centerpiece (or candlesticks) and dessert fork and/or spoon.

• Dishes should always be scraped off in the kitchen over by the sink and garbage can, *never* at the dinner table (even if you're eating in the kitchen)! If your guests insist on helping you bring dishes into the kitchen, let them, but it would be nice for you to insist that they then return to their seat instead of helping any further. They will appreciate that you want the dinner to be free of "work" for them. When you remove the plates, simply take one in each hand and head for the kitchen. Don't pile them on top of one another at the table. Something's bound to break, and besides, it looks awful. You're not at the corner coffee shop and you're not the "dishwasher." Well, actually you may be—but not until you get into the kitchen!

• When dinner is over, wait for the host or hostess to place his or her napkin on the table and stand up, before you too start to rise.

• Be sure to thank your host or hostess for the meal, complimenting him or her on whatever you found to be particularly terrific. (No need to wax poetic about everything. Remember what I said about compliments ringing false!) Whatever you do, don't say you adored something that you actually disliked. Your thoughtful host or hostess is likely to remember, and serve it to you again! (That once happened to me when I falsely complimented a peculiar-tasting chocolate mousse.) Finally, if you are the host or hostess, accept any compliments gracefully by saying, "I'm so glad you liked it!"

• Once you have stood up, push your chair in with both hands. It does not have to be tucked in completely, but just enough to keep the table from having a scattered look.

o

m

e

n

You are enjoying your salad at a wonderful dinner party when suddenly you realize you are about to pass some gas.

Try to hold it. Most times the need will pass. But if you can tell that it has to happen, excuse yourself and go to the bathroom. If you are at a restaurant and must use the rest room, you may feel uncomfortable relieving yourself in front of others, but just go into a stall and allow the gas to pass. This is the place to do it and those around you will understand—it happens to everyone.

t

• If you need at anytime to excuse yourself to visit the bathroom, simply say, very softly, "Please excuse me," stand up and leave your napkin on your chair, then walk away from the table. If everyone around you is involved in a very animated conversation, stand up and quietly leave the room. The point is, bathrooms are not a topic people like to hear about while eating. Do keep in mind that the best time to use the bathroom is in between courses.

eating etiquette

Some foods require specific table manners, if you plan on being savvy. Here are some examples.

salad

If salad is served before the entrée, then you should eat it with your salad fork and when you are through, place the fork at the four-thirty position on your plate, so that it can be taken away with your salad plate. If salad is served along with your main dish, then you may use the same fork. If the lettuce leaves have not been torn into small enough pieces, use your knife to cut them. And beware of squirting cherry tomatoes! Lightly press your knife against one side of the tomato and then pierce it with a fork. If it's a tiny cherry tomato, then lift your fork and pop the tomato into your mouth. If it's a larger one, you might want to cut it in half.

bread and butter

Using either your own or the table butter knife, slice a piece of butter from the main butter plate and place it on your own bread and butter dish next to the roll or slice of bread. Break off a small piece of bread, and butter it with the small butter knife that is perched at the top of the plate. If you do not have a special plate for your bread, you can put it down on the tablecloth to the left of your dinner plate. And if you do not have a butter knife, then use your entrée/dinner knife to butter your bread. But never use that same knife, smudged with food, to touch the butter from the table butter dish that everyone is using.

mustard, ketchup, jam, butter, sugar, and other extras

Usually if these condiments are served in dishes, they will each come with their own separate tiny spoon or knife. Be sure to use these utensils and not the spoon or knife that is at your place setting. Everyone shares the food in these small bowls, and if everyone were to use their own spoon, they would be passing around not only the mustard, but a lot of germs as well! Also, don't forget to use the utensil from each dish only for the condiment it accompanies. It isn't appetizing to see streaks of mustard in the ketchup dish! When you are through using one of these special spoons or knives, be sure to return it either

m i s e r a b l e

o

m

e

n

t

You've just started lunch when a tiny piece of chicken is caught between your teeth (or in your braces!). It's driving you crazy!

Don't go at it with your finger at the table! First try to use your tongue to remove the trapped morsel. If this doesn't work and you can tolerate the annoying feeling, then wait until a pause between courses. Excuse yourself from the table and go to the bathroom. There you can use whatever method you'd like, such as a finger (the most popular) or a toothpick, to remove the offending piece of food. (Of course, be sure to wash your hands before and after.)

m i s e r a b l e

o

m

e

n

t

While you are cutting a carrot, it torpedoes off your plate.

Use your bread and butter knife or your spoon to scoop it up and put the mischievous piece of food on either your bread and butter plate or on the side of your dinner plate. Remember, one should not use a fork or fingers. Your fork is for spearing food that goes into your mouth, and your fingers are for holding the fork.

to the correct condiment bowl or if there is a small dish under the bowl, then on that, with the utensil at the four-thirty position.

tiny bones or pits

Place the bite of fish or the olive in your mouth. Keeping your mouth closed, remove the meat from the bone or pit the olive with your teeth. Then bring your fork up to your mouth and with your tongue thrust the bone or pit onto the fork. Place it on the side of your dinner plate. Never put these things in your napkin. And fingers are forbidden.

soup

Place your spoon in the soup and push the liquid away from you. Then bring the spoon up-up-up to your mouth. If there is only a little bit of soup left in the bowl, tilt the bowl away from you and then bring the spoon up to your mouth. When you are finished with the soup, the spoon goes on the side of the plate that is under the bowl. If there is no plate underneath, then simply place the spoon in the center of the bowl with the handle at three o'clock. If the soup is very hot, don't blow on it. Wait a moment instead to let it cool, then skim the top!

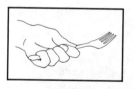

the main course or entrée

First of all, it's important to hold your knife and fork correctly. This all comes down to one important factor. *Power fingers.* Nothing looks or works worse than holding either utensil as if it were a dagger. Open your hand palm up. Place the knife or fork between the thumb and index finger. Now you have the *power*. Grasp and turn your hand over, resting your index finger along the handle.

To properly cut food, hold your knife in the hand with which you write, and your fork in the other. Pierce the part of the meat closest to you with the fork to keep it steady, and slice off a small piece with your knife. Be sure to use your index (power) fingers to keep both the knife and fork firm. When you are through cutting, place your knife down on the plate with the tip at twelve noon, switch your fork into that hand, and bring it up to your mouth. If you choose to eat "European style" (not switching back and forth), then do not place your knife down after cutting your food, and do not switch your fork to the other hand. Instead, pierce the meat with your fork in the power finger position, and bring it up to your mouth.

hot or spicy foods

If you bite into something spicy, don't immediately open your mouth wide and fan your face. Rather, take a quick sip or two of water and, if it is available, a bit of bread. If the food is simply too hot to eat, then wait for it to cool off a little before trying it again.

straws

Never bang the straw on the table as if it were a judge's gavel to remove it from the paper. Rip the end and push the paper back. Place the paper on the table beside the glass, not in an ashtray (a cigarette could start a fire). Once the straw is in your glass, remember to bring the drink up to you so that the straw comes to your mouth, not the other way around. That is, unless you want to look like a duck bobbing for food!

particular food know-how

Some foods require special savvy to eat them properly. Here are some examples.

apples and pears

If you are starting with a whole fruit, cut it into quarters. The seeds or core should be removed with your knife and fork and after that is

the ré way—the six cardinal rules of eating

• **One mouth, one cut.** If you're served a steak, don't cut off a number of pieces before you begin eating—unless of course you are fixing the plate for a three-year-old. Slice off one mouth-size bite, eat it, and then begin again.

• **Never place a utensil that has been used on the tablecloth.** It belongs on a plate. Otherwise, the area around your plate could look as if you never had one.

• **Never use your fingers to push food onto your fork,** unless you are eating a finger food such as pizza. Use your knife to assist instead.

• **Always bring your food up to your mouth.** Never bring your head down to your food or drink. No one wants to look like a bird. Besides, there is little exercise one can get while eating, so why not take advantage of the only possibility. Lift that arm!

• **Never put your elbows on the table while you are eating and always keep them close to your sides.** Held too far out from your body, they intrude on your neighbor's space and will make you look like a bird in flight. Placed on the table, they will give you the appearance of hovering protectively over your food, which doesn't look nice. After all, no one's going to steal it!

• **Respect your dinner companions and chew with your mouth closed.** One, people will lose their appetite if they have to watch your food being ground into a pulp, and two, the food might fall out of your mouth, which could leave you feeling very embarrassed and still quite hungry!

done you can eat with your fingers or fork. "European style," however, requires that you use your knife and fork till the bitter (but very sweet!) end. If the fruit is served already sliced into an attractive salad arrangement, use your fork. Fingers, in this case, are not allowed.

artichokes

This vegetable is eaten with the fingers almost all the way. Pull off one leaf at a time and dip it into the sauce that is served alongside. Then, holding on with the tips of your fingers to the top of each leaf, pull it through your teeth to "scrape" off the soft part at the other end.

When all the outer leaves have been "scraped" and arranged neatly around the side of your plate, remove the fuzzy prickly part in the middle by cutting under it and lifting it off. Make sure you don't miss any prickles! Then slice the artichoke heart into pieces (one piece at a time), dipping each piece into the sauce with your fork.

asparagus

It is so tempting to eat this with the fingers, but don't! Both the soft tips and the tender part of the stem should be eaten with your knife and fork.

bananas

Served whole at the table, the banana should be peeled all the way with the tip cut, not snapped, off. When the skin has been removed, it should be placed on your plate. The banana should be eaten by breaking off pieces with your fingers or, European style, by slicing with a knife and fork. (Whatever you do, don't make like a monkey by

m i s e r a b l e

o
m
e
n
t

Your friend's parents have taken you and him out to dinner and you make the mistake of opening your mouth to talk while it is still full. Some food falls out and your friend laughs uproariously.

First of all, recognize that your friend's social savvy is in a state of disrepair. He needs help. Try not to let him embarrass you. After all, he's partly responsible for this uncomfortable scene. He's made an embarrassing situation feel worse than it has to. Promptly close your mouth again and finish chewing the contents while at the same time using your spoon or knife to pick up the mischievous piece of food (unless it landed on the floor).

Place the morsel on your plate and then do one of two things. Pretend it never happened, or smile nicely at your host and hostess and say, "Sorry about that" or "Excuse me." They'll understand. It happens to everyone.

chomping away at a half-peeled banana with the skin draping over your fingers and wrist!)

chili

Eat it with a spoon!

clams on the half shell

Use your seafood fork (or if you don't have one, your salad fork) to pry the clam out of the half shell. If you want to add horseradish or sauce, put a bit right onto the clam in the shell and then pull the whole thing out. The same goes for oysters.

clams (steamed)

Using your fingers, lift out each clam by its neck, then pull the body loose and discard the dark neck part. Dip the clam (if you choose) in melted butter and eat in one bite.

---

finger foods

I've spent a lot of time impressing upon you the fact that only a few foods can be eaten with the fingers. Here is a list of some of the most popular foods in the category. And remember this: When in doubt, use your knife and fork. Any way you "cut it," you will always look good, and offend no one.

Bread Sticks	Corn on the Cob	Grapes	Pizza
Carrot and Celery Stalks	Small Egg Rolls	Hamburgers *	Sandwiches **
	Frankfurters	Ice-Cream Pops	Toast
Cheese Wedges	French Fries	Nacho Chips and	
Cookies	Fried Chicken	Dip	

* It's neater to cut these in half first with a knife and fork.
** Hot gravy sandwiches should, of course, always be eaten with a knife and fork.

---

corn on the cob

Put the ear of corn on your dinner plate, and use your butter knife to spread butter all over. Lift the corn to your mouth with both hands and nibble away in horizontal lines. Sometimes your corn will be served with cob holders. These do tend to keep your fingers dry, but the butter can still drip downward, so keep that napkin on your lap!

fried chicken

This is one of those foods people assume is a finger food but in fact may not be. The deciding factor is where it is served. On a picnic, certainly, you can go right ahead and pick it up with your hands. But otherwise, steady the piece of chicken on your plate with a fork in one hand and then with your other, cut away the meat with a knife.

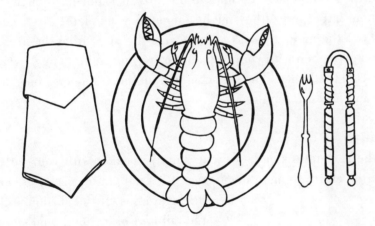

lobster

This is always served with a tool that looks like a nutcracker. You use it to crack the two big claws first. Then you break them apart further with both hands. Next, pick up one of the claws and with a seafood fork dig out the meat, placing it on your plate to cut it into bite-sized pieces. Finally, dip it in melted butter (though I like mine sweet and plain) and taste your rich reward for all that hard work! To get meat out of the small claws, break them with your fingers and either suck out the meat or dig it out with your fork. The coral-colored or green roe of the lobster are eaten with a fork. To eat the tail, simply cut down the middle with a knife and fork and pull it out before you cut it up. And if you want, put on that bib! No one can eat a lobster neatly, though everyone should try.

peas

Despite the fact that you might be tempted to pick up these slippery little things with a spoon, *always* use a fork. If there are a few stubborn peas that refuse to be caught, use your knife to nudge them onto your fork. This works great for rice as well.

rock cornish hens

No, these hens have nothing to do with rock music, though if you cut them improperly, they might dance off your plate! First, cut the hen down the middle. Work on removing the meat from the breast by steadying the hen with your fork and using your knife to peel away the meat from the bones. The legs can be a bit more slippery, but, alas, a knife and fork are required here too.

shrimp

If the shrimp is small, you can simply spear it with your fork and plunk the entire thing into your mouth. If it's jumbo size, you can eat it in two bites. If the shrimp still has the tail part of its shell, you can pick it up with your fingers, or use your knife and fork.

m i s e r a b l e

o m e n t

Your friend across the table has some food stuck to her chin, but she doesn't know it. You'd like to tell her without embarrassing her in front of others.

Get her attention with your eyes, and then with a napkin, brush off your chin as if the food were on you. Chances are she will get the hint.

snails

These delicacies are served in their shells. They are cooked with a buttery garlic sauce, which you won't want to miss. First, with the special

social savvy

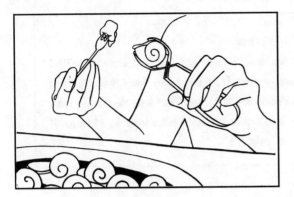

You have ordered an entrée that comes with a lemon. You squeeze it over your fish, but instead it squirts onto your neighbor's plate.

First, apologize. Then remind yourself it isn't a tragedy. Finally, remember for next time the better way. Pierce the middle of the lemon with your fork and at the same time with your other hand squeeze the two ends. Do remember to use the hand that is squeezing for a cover. That way you can be sure your neighbor won't be treated to a "sour shower."

metal clamps provided, pick up and hold the shell. (They are served *hot!*) With your other hand (the one you write with), pull out the snail with a seafood fork and eat it in one bite. If you would like to finish up the tasty liquid in each shell, you could dip small pieces of bread inside with your fork.

spaghetti

Long spaghetti should be twirled around your fork, not cut up with your knife. Start twirling a small amount of spaghetti either on a fork alone or, as some people prefer, on a fork held with the tines against the inside of a spoon. Then keep twirling, to avoid spaghetti whiplash! Who needs those stray strands flapping about sending sauce every which way! When the last strand is completely wound, put the whole thing in your mouth.

stews

These should be eaten with a fork. Liquid can be soaked up with pieces of bread. Break the bread into the bowl and use your fork to swirl the pieces around.

This chapter has essentially been about *know-how*. It has been filled with the how-tos of mealtime savoir faire. But make no mistake about it—this chapter has also touched on all the building blocks I spoke of in Chapter Two. It has explored being *sensitive* to others at the table, *compromising* to be sure everyone has what they need, taking *responsibility* for your part in making the meal pleasant, and *respecting* the right that others have to enjoy the food. When it comes to sitting down to a great meal, table-time *know-how* is your ticket to social savvy.

dining out

*L*ots of people view restaurant dining as an adventure. I must confess I am one of them for several reasons. It can be a splendid opportunity to try new foods that aren't usually served at home. It affords me the perfect opportunity to dress up and visit a new and interesting place. And I find it rather exciting to be in a room with lots of people I've never seen before. The energy and activity in a restaurant can be a wonderful thing to experience.

And let's not forget about those five senses I mentioned in the last chapter. Think of all the things there are to see (the decor), touch (the fine linen and crusty bread), smell (the delicious aromas coming from so many different dishes), taste (the hors d'oeuvres, the main course, the dessert), and hear (snippets of conversation from the table next to yours, a waiter's exotic French, Chinese, or Greek accent!). Naturally, all the table manners we covered in the previous chapter apply to dining both at home and at a restaurant. But here is your chance to display not only those manners, but also some special and sophisticated *know-how*. In public, no less!

A restaurant is a small world unto itself. And as with any new place, it's a good idea to know your way around. Let this chapter serve as a kind of travel guide. You'll discover how to plan ahead, make reservations, follow the customs (sitting on the floor in a Japanese restaurant, for instance), speak a few words in different languages, and tip appropriately! Consider dining out an adventure. Any surprises that come along will not only be manageable, but also fun!

selecting a restaurant

What kind of food are you in the mood for? Good burgers? Italian? Chinese? What sort of place would you like to go to? Casual? Dressy? Entertaining? Quiet? How much money would you like to spend? Is it no object? Are you on a very tight budget? Do you need quick service? Are you trying to catch a movie or can you eat slowly?

All of these questions and more are the kinds of things you should ask yourself when choosing a place to dine. This is so for one very good reason: The restaurant will not and cannot change anything about itself for you. If the food is Italian, it's likely they will not serve French onion soup. If the place is dressy, you cannot wear jeans. If the meals are expensive, they will not slash a few dollars off the price to suit your wallet, and if the service is leisurely, it is unlikely that they will purchase roller skates for the chef and waiter!

Quite simply, you must go to a place that *is* what you want. You cannot expect to make it so. Well, you might say, "How do I know all these things without first going there?" Good question. Here are some suggestions.

• Restaurant reviews in local papers or big city restaurant guides will usually tell you the style of the restaurant, the price range of the dishes, and the sort of food that is served.
• Speaking to people you know who have dined at a particular restaurant is both helpful and wise. After all, they have nothing to lose by telling you the complete truth! (Keep in mind, however, that what tastes good to one person may not be nearly as appetizing to another!) Ask them about the food, dress, prices, atmosphere, service, and anything else you would like to know.
• If you can't find any reviews or know no one who has dined at a particular place, call the restaurant. It is perfectly fine to ask if the dress is casual or if the place is noisy or quiet. And for a general idea about price, "Could you tell me the price range for your entrées" would be just fine. I wouldn't advise asking if the service is slow. No

one will say yes to that question. But you might say, "We have a film to catch. Do you think we can expect to be out quickly?"

The key, then, to enjoying a restaurant is knowing the sort of place you need before you make your choice.

making your reservations

Many popular restaurants, especially on the weekends, require reservations. You might need to call as early as a week in advance (though for most places a day or two ahead will do nicely). It depends on the size, popularity, and policy of the restaurant. Making a reservation is a very simple procedure that goes something like this.

(Phone rings.) "Good afternoon. Leo's Seafood."
"Hello. I'd like to make a reservation for this Saturday evening."
"What's the name, please?"
"Cutler." (Give only your last name.)
"What time?"
"Seven-thirty, please."
"How many will you be?"
"Two, please." (Or however many you will be.)
"That will be two for dinner at seven-thirty, Saturday evening."
"Yes, thank you." (At this point you can ask for directions or information on parking.)
"Fine. Have a nice day."

And that's that. Some restaurants that take reservations days in advance may ask you for your number, as they will want to call that Saturday afternoon to make sure you will indeed be coming. If you would rather not give the number, then simply say you will be unreachable. Most restaurants will hold your reservation for only fifteen minutes to a half hour. So don't be late. Unless you like eating late, of course—after everyone else with a reservation has dined!

A final word about reservations: Many people make reservations and then without calling to cancel decide to go elsewhere. This is not fair. The restaurant will hold your table for a while, thereby slowing up other people who might like to take a seat. Those who are waiting might even opt to leave. Thus the restaurant loses out on serving them a meal. If you change your mind, be considerate and *responsible*. Call and cancel.

walking in

Once you walk in from the street, you may notice a coat check. This is a little room managed by someone who takes your coat and gives you in return a "check" or tag that bears the number of the hanger upon which your coat will be hanging. In more casual restaurants, however, there may be only a coatrack available to everyone. In either situation, coat check or coatrack, the gentleman should always ask his female companion if he can take care of her coat. The one exception to this is furs. Most adults prefer to drape their furs on the backs of their seats, where they can keep an eye on them. (Some people even ask for an extra chair just for the coat! No menu, though.) Coat-check rooms are not insured. If the coat is stolen, it is not the responsibility of the restaurant.

meeting the maître d'

Once you are no longer with coat, you will be greeted by the maître d'. This may be a man or a woman, often quite elegantly dressed (depending on the restaurant). He or she is available to greet you, bid you farewell, and to assist with any problems in between. Other than that, it's your waiter to whom you will be speaking. The maître d' will ask if you have a reservation. If you do, he or she will take you to your table (with perhaps a small delay if the table needs to be cleared). If you do not have a reservation and there are no tables available, he or she will tell you how long the wait is, and then it is up to you to decide whether or not to stay. Once the maître d' has led you to your table, he or she might help the ladies with their chairs and then distribute menus. Before leaving your table, he or she will likely tell you that the waiter will be right with you and then wish you a good meal. A simple "Thank you" on your part will do nicely as a response.

"taking" your table

Now, suppose you have arrived at your table and you don't like it. Perhaps it's too close to the waiter's station where dishes are piled or water is poured. Perhaps it's right on top of the kitchen's swinging door. Or maybe it's simply too close to the bar and thus much too noisy. Do you have to accept it? If you've made a reservation, usually not. Politely turn to the maître d' and say something like, "I'm sorry, but we feel this table is too close to the kitchen. Do you think we might be seated at another further away?" Or, "This section of the restaurant is a bit too noisy for us. May we have a table more toward the back, please?" Chances are he will be able to satisfy your needs, if not immediately, then soon after. Be aware that you may have to return to the waiting area until another table is free. The couple that was next in line after you will likely be led to the table you just rejected. However, if you do not have a reservation, you might have to stay where you are for quite a while, in which case you may choose to leave.

In terms of seating, boy-girl-boy-girl is best. The person who has done the inviting (if this evening is a treat) should sit facing into the restaurant, so he or she can easily draw the attention of the waiter. Women, also, should be seated facing into the restaurant, if possible. It's nicer to look at the decor than the wall!

meeting your waiter

After a moment or two your waiter will approach the table, fill your glass with water (if there isn't a drought!), introduce himself, and take

miserable moment

You are sitting in a nonsmoking area and someone lights up. Already you can smell the smoke and it really bothers you.

The person who is smoking is doing so against restaurant policy. Chances are a waiter or the manager will notice and immediately request that he or she snuff out the cigarette. However, if it does go unnoticed, call over your waiter and in a quiet voice draw his attention to the matter. It is sufficient to say, "Excuse me, but this is a nonsmoking area and the person at the next table is smoking. It does bother me, so would you please take care of it."

You may get an angry look from the smoker, but rules are rules. Of course, if you are seated in a smoking section, you have two choices. You could nicely ask the person yourself to blow the smoke in the other direction (which this person does not have to do, and even if he or she tries, it may not work) or you could ask the waiter to switch you to another table. In other words, in this situation it's your problem.

a drink order. He will say something like, "Hello. My name is Frank. I will be your waiter this evening," or simply, "Hello. I am your waiter. Will you be having drinks this evening?"

When the drink arrives, the waiter may put it on your entrée plate or above your plate on the upper right-hand side. If he does place it on your plate, after you take the first sip, you can place it on the table on the upper right-hand side of your plate.

At this point, before the waiter walks away, and if he hasn't done so already, you might say, "May we please have a menu?"

translating a menu

Menus are divided into sections. These sections often depend on the type of restaurant. Almost all menus include a section labeled appetizers or hors d'oeuvres, another labeled main courses or entrées, and another labeled for desserts. Some menus have a separate listing for soups and another for vegetables (if they do not come automatically with the main course). Still other menus divide up their main courses under various categories such as pasta, fish, poultry, and meat. And then of course there are the specials, which are sometimes printed on small cards and clipped onto the menu, or a "special dinner," which may offer a specific combination of hors d'oeuvre, entrée, and dessert for a certain price. It sounds confusing, but once you see the menu, it probably won't be. Still, I would never claim that all menus are perfectly clear! Some *are* confusing. If you are not sure if vegetables come with the main dish or if the appetizer is included in the price of the "House Special Dinner," then ask your waiter. "Excuse me. I'm not sure I understand the menu" would be just fine.

One other point: Sometimes the specials are not noted on the menu. The waiter will simply approach your table and say, "May I tell you about our specials?" And then he will proceed (usually much too quickly!) to list the appetizers, soup, pasta, and/or meat dish that the chef has concocted just for that evening. Listen to him (don't start chatting with your neighbors), but don't get nervous. It's not a test! You can always ask him to repeat something before he walks away, or when he returns to take your order.

ordering dinner

"May I take your order?" the waiter will say, standing by your table, pad and pen in hand. "Yes, we are ready," someone will say.

At this point you can order in either of two ways. Your host or hostess can order for everyone (once he or she knows what you would like, of course) or the waiter can go around the table giving each person a chance to speak. First the appetizer is ordered and then the main course, with sometimes a soup or salad in between. The waiter will return after the main dish has been cleared to take your dessert

In fancier restaurants there is often more than just a waiter serving you. Often there is a busboy or extra server, wearing more simple dress than the waiter, whose job it is to place butter on your bread and butter plate and fill your glass with water. He might also be the one to replace your napkin or silverware if either falls on the floor and to clear the crumbs off your table at the end of the meal. He is not the person who takes your order, though you can request that he send over your waiter.

order. The one exception to this is a special dessert such as flambé, which may need an extended period of time to be prepared. You would, in this case, place your order when you choose your entrée.

When it is your turn to order, there are several questions you are more than entitled to ask the waiter before you commit to any one dish. Here are some typical examples.

• "Could you please repeat the———special?"
• "Could you please tell me the price of the———special?" Often prices are not mentioned with the specials. You are certainly entitled to know the cost of anything you order, even if you're the guest, in which case you may not want to request a very expensive item. The one exception might be if you are being taken out to a very fancy restaurant and it's clear that price is no object.
• "Could you please tell me how the ———is prepared?" If you don't like heavy cream sauces, for example, or do not like the taste of capers, this is a way of not being unpleasantly surprised when your dish arrives.
• "Is it possible to have a red, instead of white, sauce on the noodles?" It is perfectly all right to ask whether or not the chef can prepare your food in a slightly different manner. But if the waiter says no, it is not okay to argue. Still, there are a few requests you can make with which few chefs would have a problem. A few examples are: broiled fish without butter; salad dressing on the side instead of mixed in; a baked potato instead of mashed; a spicy dish, spiced lightly.
• "I don't see hamburgers on your menu, but might I have one?" You may ask for something simple that you do not see on the menu, such as a hamburger or a plain piece of broiled chicken, but do understand many restaurants will only serve what is on the menu. If this is the case, then the waiter might suggest something on the menu that is close to what you desire, such as Salisbury steak, which is much like a hamburger.
• "Could you please tell me what 'florentine' means?" Often you may find yourself looking at a French, Italian, or Spanish menu. Many

words may look unfamiliar. Don't be afraid or embarrassed to ask the waiter for help. That's a lot easier for him than having to return a dish to the kitchen because you had no idea that "florentine" means "with spinach"!

Which brings me to my next point. I thought it might be helpful to include a menu glossary here. Listed are some key words you will likely find on French, Italian, and Spanish menus and what they mean. Obviously, I have included only some of the words and dishes you are apt to see, but I hope it's just enough to keep you from feeling like a total "foreigner" when you pick up the menu!

---

french

Quiche Lorraine: Cheese pie.

Caviar: The eggs or roe of a large fish, usually sturgeon. Caviar is customarily served as an appetizer.

Coquilles Saint Jacques à la Crème: Scallops with cream.

Béchamel Sauce: Sauce made of butter, flour, milk, a dash of nutmeg (a white sauce).

Béarnaise Sauce: Sauce made of butter, eggs, vinegar, parsley. Traditionally served with broiled red meat, especially steak.

Hollandaise Sauce: Yellow-colored sauce, made of butter and eggs. Used for eggs Benedict or over asparagus.

Vinaigrette: Dressing made of salt, pepper, vinegar, oil, mustard, chopped herbs. Served over salads and some vegetables.

Crêpes: Very thin French pancakes. Filled with anything from meat, chicken, or fish to dessert fillings.

Ratatouille: Medley of vegetables with a tomato base.

Flambé: A dessert that liqueur is poured over. The concoction is lit, then served hot after the flame dies down.

Bouillabaisse: A soup made with shellfish and fish that is poured over oven-toasted bread.

Mousse au Chocolat: A heavy and rich chocolate pudding.

---

italian

Scaloppine alla Marsala: Sauteed veal scallops with marsala (wine) sauce.

Minestrone Soup: A vegetable soup with chicken flavoring containing beans, potatoes, celery, carrots, and noodles.

Veal Parmigiana: Breaded veal with a tomato sauce, topped with mozzarella cheese.

Antipasti or *Antipasto:* An appetizer salad, often with olives, fish, ham, sausage, and vegetables both raw and cooked. Usually topped with oil and vinegar dressing.

Fettucine Alfredo: Broad noodles tossed with a heavy cream sauce.

Spaghetti alla Carbonara: Spaghetti with a cream sauce that includes ham.

Lasagne: Baked layers of wide pasta, with tomato sauce and ricotta cheese.

Ricotta Cheese: A white, creamy cheese often used in pasta dishes.

Scampi: Shrimp, baked in the oven or fried.

Zabaione: A wine-and-egg custard.

Spumoni: Italian ice cream.

spanish

Gazpacho: A cold soup made with tomatoes, cucumber, green peppers, onion, and garlic.

Paella: Saffron (yellow) rice mixed with some combination of fish, shellfish, chicken, to-matoes, and peas.

Flan: A dessert of caramel custard.

Arroz con Pollo: Chicken and rice.

enjoying the food

Your food has just arrived. With a proud flourish your waiter places the dish before you. He may say, "It's hot." Don't bother testing the fact by placing your hands on the plate and then waving them in the air to cool them off. He knows what he's talking about and you'll look a bit silly! Glance around the table, wait for everyone who has ordered an appetizer (not everyone does!) to be served, and then pick up your fork. If it's tasty, have a great time. But if it isn't, here's what you can do.

problem food

The appetizer is not at all what you expected. (Perhaps the sauce is too spicy, or the preparation too greasy.)

m i s e r a b l e

o *You're sitting, and sitting, and sitting, but the waiter just won't come to take your*

m *order.*

e *That's simple. Just get up, walk over to the maître d' or the manager, and tell him*

n *or her the problem. You can bet the waiter will be there in no time flat.*

t

Sometimes you can tell if there is a problem simply by looking at the dish. In this case, you can call the waiter over by catching his eye or raising your hand slightly when he looks in your direction. Very nicely and quietly say something like, "This is not what I thought it was going to be. May I return this and see a menu, please?" However, if you have already taken a bite, you might first want to see if anyone at the table would like to switch with you. (I usually suggest that this option be reserved for family members only.) If not, politely ask the waiter for a change. But be sure that you stopped at that *one* bite. It's neither right nor fair to return a half-eaten dish with the complaint that it wasn't what you expected. The same goes for a main dish. If it

---

how to catch a waiter's attention

- Wait until he looks in your direction and then nod slightly.
- Wait until he looks in your direction and then raise one hand slightly.
- Wait until he is within earshot and, whether or not he is looking, say, "Excuse me, waiter?"

Never shout across the room, "Oh, waiter!" You're not at a baseball game looking for hot dogs.

---

doesn't look or taste appetizing to you, return it. But this time don't ask if anyone would like to switch. Most people are more committed to their choice of main dish than appetizer.

The appetizer or main dish is not prepared the way you specifically asked.

If you gave the waiter your order with some specific requests and he nodded his understanding, then you have a right to expect the dish will arrive properly prepared. Do not, however, use a whiny or angry voice! Simply call the waiter over and remind him of your request by saying something like, "Excuse me, but I did want this steak cooked rare," or, "May I please have my salad with the dressing on the side as I ordered?" He will most certainly take the dish back to the kitchen and return in a short while (hopefully) with a correctly prepared meal. (If it is your dinner partner who is returning a dish, you might want to request a metal cover for your hot food to keep it warm while your friend awaits his or her meal.)

while dining

During the course of your meal, you might have a number of quite common requests. Here is how to handle them.

You want more bread for the basket.

m i s e r a b l e m o m e n t

You've ordered your food ages ago and nothing has come out of the kitchen. You're starving and you have a movie to catch.

Catch your waiter's attention and politely ask him what's taking so long. "We've been waiting a long time for our meal. Is there a problem?" will suffice. You might also add that you are trying to make a movie. If it's a terribly busy restaurant, he may have lost track of who ordered what when, and the kitchen itself might be confused and a little behind. By reminding the waiter of your presence (and impatience), he will most probably take immediate action, which in this case means going into the kitchen to find out what's going on with your order. Chances are your food will be out quickly.

When the person who fills your water glass or a waiter passes by, simply say, "Excuse me. May we please have more bread?" When it arrives, just say thank you. If it is not your waiter, you can either ask him to send yours over or simply say, "Could you please tell our waiter we'd like more bread?"

You want directions to the rest rooms.

It's most polite to excuse yourself from the table, approach a waiter or the maître d', who is usually at the entrance of the dining room, and ask for directions.

You want a fresh fork or napkin.

If either item falls on the floor, simply catch your waiter's eye and politely ask for a replacement. Many people pass in and out of the restaurant, and while certainly you can assume a degree of cleanliness, you are entitled to use only freshly cleaned utensils and linens. (Please don't be embarrassed about dropping something. It happens to everyone.)

You want a waiter to stop hovering.

Some waiters think that by standing near your table throughout the meal, they are doing a great job. This isn't so, though I confess it's not for you to deliver that lecture. The truth is, the best waiters are those who are there when you need them and are seemingly gone when you don't. It can be very uncomfortable to have what is essentially a stranger lurking about. If this happens to you, catch his attention with your eyes and when he approaches, quietly say, "If we need you, we will let you know." It's a *sensitive* approach and he will get the point.

You want the table cleared.

Most often a waiter will notice when you are through with whatever course you have been served. You can help him along by placing your fork and knife at the four-thirty position on your plate. But if he doesn't, you may call him over and say something like, "It was delicious." The plates will disappear. But, watch out! Especially in fancy restaurants, something new will appear! The waiter or busboy will use a crumber, which is a curved flat piece of metal, to brush off the crumbs around your plate. Don't feel embarrassed! The crumber was invented to keep your table clean for the next course.

basic restaurant conduct

When you are dining out, you are surrounded by other people. You are all sharing the same space and even some of the same waiters. In order for the experience to be a pleasant one, everyone has to be

social savvy

considerate and *respectful* of everyone else. To this end there are a few "rules of conduct" to keep in mind.

• Don't stare at other people as they are eating. Strangers can often be quite interesting to watch, but think about how you would feel with a pair of eyes boring into you. Be considerate and allow people at nearby tables to have some privacy.

• Keep your voice down. There are always those who love to eavesdrop, but most would prefer not to hear everything you have to say. Loud voices and laughing make it difficult for people to talk and think. This isn't fair. Everyone comes to a restaurant to enjoy the food and pleasant conversation. But they only want to enjoy theirs, not yours! *Respect* their privacy.

m i s e r a b l e
o
m
e
n
t

You reach for a piece of bread from the bread basket and in so doing knock over your glass of water.

Don't freeze! It may feel like everyone in the restaurant is looking, but they aren't! First take your napkin off your lap and place it over the spreading wet spot on the tablecloth. In this way you will protect not only your own clothes but those of the person sitting next to you. Then catch the waiter's eye and tell him what has happened. He will offer you a fresh napkin, blot up the excess water with yet another napkin, place a fresh one on the wet spot, and finally quietly disappear. This kind of accident is commonplace in restaurants! (If the water has gotten onto your main dish, he should quickly take the dish away and in the kitchen place the food on a fresh plate.)

• Don't try to draw people at nearby tables into conversation unless they invite it. Most times people would rather be left alone with their dinner companions. It's a funny thing about restaurants. People often go there to be alone. Sometimes the best place to be alone is one where you are surrounded by strangers.

Note: If you notice your neighbors are eating something that looks wonderful, don't ask them about it! When it's time for you to order, ask your waiter to identify the dish.

• Don't interrupt your waiter while he is taking an order from the next table. He needs to concentrate on what he is doing, and those people have a right to his complete attention. Whatever it is you need can surely wait until he is through.

• When you slide in or out of your table to use the rest room or even at the conclusion of your meal, *be careful*. If the tables are close together, you could easily knock over someone's water glass or silverware. If you are carrying anything, use a little *know-how* and move slowly, keeping it close to your side.

ordering dessert

Once the table is clean, the waiter will offer coffee or tea, and give out dessert menus, recite the available desserts, or wheel over the dessert cart. If you cannot clearly see an interesting dessert on this cart, then simply ask the waiter to bring the particular tart or cake a little closer. You may ask him to describe in detail what sort of cream filling is in the cake, or fruit in the tart. If there is nothing on the cart that appeals to you, you might want to ask if he can offer you a small fruit platter. Most restaurants can easily accommodate this request.

Many people like to share desserts. If this is your choice, then select a cake, tart, or pie (you can't split a parfait!). Inform the waiter of your intentions and he will slice the dessert in half and serve it with two plates and forks.

m i s e r a b l e

o

m

You're not quite through with your meal, but the waiter has now walked over and is about to take your plate away.

e

n

t

Stop him. It may not feel comfortable, but it's a lot better than allowing him to walk off with your food while you're still eating. Say something like, "Excuse me, but I'm not quite finished." He will likely apologize and move away rather embarrassed—which is why you shouldn't cry out, *"Stop!* I'm not finished!" He will most probably feel awkward enough!

You think you are next in line at the pizza shop. The person behind the counter says, "Who's next?" You are in the middle of replying "Two slices with . . ." when suddenly a woman standing next to you interrupts, "Excuse me! Don't you have any manners! It was my turn!"

People who confront others in this manner (and there are many) are actually quite rude themselves. After all, there are other ways to tell a person they're out of turn. It almost doesn't matter if she is right or wrong. It can be very embarrassing to be confronted in public like that, and often it can make you feel "wrong" even if you aren't! If in truth you suspect she is correct, the easiest way to handle this is to step back, smile apologetically, and simply say,

"I'm sorry. I didn't realize you were before me." You won't have to answer the question about your manners. The answer will be obvious. If, however, you think you're right, you have two basic choices. You could argue politely by saying "I'm sorry, you're wrong" and hold your ground. But that might invite her to loudly complain about how it's really her turn, and to speculate about which barn you were brought up in anyway. Your other choice is to step back and say, "I actually think I was here first, but if you insist, please go right ahead and order before me." In this way you will have gently made your point (it doesn't feel good to ignore the facts) and also avoid any further unpleasant conversation. That is very savvy.

paying the check

When the bill is brought to your table, it may be placed face down on the table, on it's own plate, or inside a long and narrow leather-type cover. There is an element of privacy involved, because the waiter may not know for sure who is paying for the meal. If everyone is paying for themselves, then the bill can be openly shared at the table. But if the dinner is a treat, then the person paying would probably not want his or her guests to see the bill. The waiter usually places the check in front of that person who looks to him to be in charge. Sometimes he's right; sometimes he's wrong. He may correctly assume the person who ordered for everyone or who ordered the wine will pay the check. (Waiters and waitresses alike often assume the man at the table is paying instead of the woman—but in fact they are often incorrect!) If you are treating, one way to make sure you get the check is to excuse yourself as if you were going to the rest room and tell the maître d' that you would like the bill to come to you. If the check is placed in front of your friend, but you in fact are treating, you might do one of two things. Either quickly say to the waiter, "I'll take that," and allow him to hand it over to you, or place your hand gently on top of the check and slide it toward you, saying to your friend, "My treat."

Many friends go out Dutch treat. This means everyone pays for themselves. This is easy to handle if there are just two of you. Simply ask the waiter for two checks. Of course, if there are several people at the table, it isn't fair to ask him to write up separate checks for everyone (unless you're at a coffee shop!). The easiest thing to do is simply to divide the check plus tip by as many number of people at the table. The only problem with this, of course, is if one or two people ordered much less expensive food than the others. Splitting the check in this situation can be a bit unfair. It would be wise to do some quick calculations in your head and take a few dollars off their shares.

other check issues

• When you receive your check, feel free to take your time going over the figures. Don't go so far as to take out a calculator. That would look a bit too distrustful! And just because everyone is paying for themselves doesn't mean everyone needs to check the bill. One or two people is enough.

• If there is a mistake on your check, simply call the waiter over and point out where you think there might be a problem. You may request a menu to check a price or to simply show him the error. Be sure to do so evenly and nicely. Mistakes on restaurant checks are not intentional.

```
how to ask for the bill
```

how to ask for the bill
- **Wait until you've caught your waiter's eye and then mouth the words, "The check, please."**
- **Wait until you've caught your waiter's eye and then raise the palm of one hand slightly and pretend to write on it with the index finger of your other hand.**
- **As your waiter passes by, catch his attention by saying, "Excuse me, but we'd like our check now, please."**

• The tip should be 15 to 20 percent of the total. However, if service has been terrible and slow, and the food quite poor, you needn't feel compelled to leave a 15 percent tip. But on your way out be sure to tell either the maître d' or the manager why you have not done so. It's not a question of offering an excuse as much as it is an opportunity to make it clear there are problems in the restaurant that need to be corrected.

taking your leave

Some people adore lingering over a cup of coffee or tea after dessert. It feels luxurious to sit in an attractive and interesting new place and simply chat quietly with friends. If the hour is late and there are no people waiting for tables, this is usually fine. But in many very popular restaurants, especially in the early evening, you may notice a line at the door. This does not, of course, mean that you should rush through your meal. In fact, quite the opposite. You are paying for a pleasant dining experience for which there should be no formal time limits. *However*, it's savvy to be reasonable. Yes, you will probably never see these people who are standing in line again, but that doesn't mean you should completely ignore their needs (they're hungry!) or those of the restaurant (it is a money-making establishment). So have that cup of tea if you would like. But don't extend your stay unnecessarily. If you want to keep talking to your companions, invite them home to your house! That is a very savvy *compromise*.

If you enjoyed your meal, it would be nice to approach the maître d' on the way out and say so. "Thank you. The meal was excellent" would be perfectly fine.

the coat check

On your way out give the coat-check tag that was handed to you earlier back to the person behind the counter. Once he or she hands you your coat, it is expected that you will leave fifty cents to a dollar in the dish that is usually sitting on the counter. If you have misplaced the small tag (which happens to lots of people), describe the coat (and any extras such as a scarf) as best as you can. If there are several people behind you waiting for coats, step aside and let them go first. It's not their fault you lost the tag, and your coat may take a while to find.

A restaurant is a wonderful place to socialize. Everything about it—the food, the decor, the strangers sitting near you, the people who serve, and even the pleasant "busy" noises going on all around contribute to a kind of excitement. Still, there are, as you can see, bits of *know-how* that are good to be familiar with before you can completely enjoy the experience. Like anything else, the more savvy you are, the more relaxed you will feel. The less you have to worry about dealing with waiters, reading menus, ordering food, and paying the check, the more you will enjoy the food, *respect* the company, and *responsibly* handle the restaurant experience. And let's face it—restaurants cost money. If you're going to spend it, why not be sure you enjoy yourself!

m i s e r a b l e   o m e n t

The bill has arrived. You've checked it over and given the waiter a large bill, expecting to get back quite a bit of change from which you will leave his tip. But it's been quite a while since he walked off, and you suddenly realize he thinks the entire amount of change is his tip.

His mistake. Unfortunately, it's placed you in an uncomfortable position. But that doesn't mean you should just let it go. Assuming the change is quite a bit over the 15 percent we discussed earlier, then call the waiter over and say, "Excuse me. But may we have our change?" You needn't spell it out any further. He may be a bit startled, but perhaps he will go home and practice up on a bit of basic math.

partying with confidence

*W*hen we think of a party, a room filled with people having fun usually comes to mind. There may be music. The room may be brightly lit. Tables with food may line the walls, and all sorts of different conversations may be going on. What fun! How relaxed and inviting everything looks! It can feel absolutely magical when a group of people come together in such a warm and often exciting way.

But guess what? It isn't magic. The truth is, most good parties need two things—and a magician isn't one of them. They need careful savvy planning and cooperative savvy guests. Careful planning will make your guests feel welcome and important. Cooperative guests will make one another feel appreciated and their host or hostess feel relaxed and successful.

In a way a party is everyone's *responsibility*. Everyone plays an important part because each person contributes to the spirit of the event. So whether you are giving a party or attending one, here's how to do your share.

giving a party: the planning stage

Creating the invitations, shopping for the food, designing decorations—preparing for a party you are giving can sometimes be as much fun as the party itself! And why not? Your party will reflect your humor, warmth, and generosity—especially if you take the time to focus on every detail.

decide on a party theme

There are many kinds of parties and even more reasons to give them. Dinner parties, tennis parties, swim parties, lunch parties, and brunch parties are only a few examples of the kind of party you might like to give. Then, there are the reasons. Birthday, Halloween, End of School, Prom, New Year's Eve, Congratulations on the Big Basketball Win, No Reason At All, and Camp Reunion are just a few possibilities. See what I mean? You can give any sort of party for any sort of reason. But you need to decide the kind and the reason well in advance. The guest list, budget, decorations, food, invitations, and entertainment also need to be carefully planned. After all, you can't send out invitations for a lunch party and then decide moments before your guests arrive that bowls of snack food will have to do!

So plan ahead. It will keep you from wasting time and ensure that your friends are thoughtfully treated.

consider your budget

I would never say that you have to let your budget alone determine the kind of party you give. That is why I have brought up the issue of budget second. *However*, your budget will have a lot to do with every aspect of planning. Invitations can be store-bought, homemade, or delivered by word of mouth. Dinner parties might feature lamb chops or much less expensive pasta. Decorations may involve fancy streamers, tablecloths, and elaborate ornaments or just soft lighting with pretty candles. The point is, if you want to give a party, money issues should not have to stop you, but you will have to adjust the details in accordance with your budget. So before you invite anyone, check your funds and discuss the matter with your parents. Are they willing to pay for the whole thing? Will part of it be a loan? Are they troubled by your spending all your savings on a party? Also, talk to your friends. Are they willing to each bring a little something (such as a bottle of soda or chips) in order to help you with the costs? These questions will play a big part in how you design your own party. Still, no matter how much money you have, in order to spend it wisely, do set a budget. The categories might be:

- Invitations
  (and postage)
- Food
- Decorations
- Party favors
- Entertainment

decide whom to invite

Now that you know the kind of party you would like to give and the amount of money you have to spend, it's time to consider who will be there! Will it be only a few close friends or all the people at school with whom you are friendly? Perhaps your party was planned for a purpose such as introducing camp friends to school friends or celebrating a swim meet. In these instances your guest list should be quite clear, give or take a few people. But no matter whom you invite, there are a few things you should keep in mind. (It would seem that since you're giving the party, you ought to be able to invite whomever you please. Unfortunately, things don't always work out that way.)

- If you're inviting a particular "crowd" to a party, you cannot leave out the one or two people you don't like very much. It would be terribly embarrassing for them and uncomfortable for their invited friends.
- If you are inviting both boys and girls, try to keep the numbers as equal as possible.
- If you have attended a party given by someone whom you don't like very much, you should return the favor. However, it isn't necessary to

invite someone with whom you don't feel comfortable to a small party. Wait until you throw a bigger "to-do" and then return the invitation.

• If you are giving a party in honor of someone else, make an effort to invite the people with whom this person is close. In this instance, your buddies are not as important as his or hers, and they will understand if they are not included this one time. Simply tell them the truth.

• If you would like to invite a person your parents do not want in their home, you might decide to keep the party quite small. In this way he or she will not feel as left out.

m i s e r a b l e o m e n t

You are throwing a party and have now given out all the invitations. Suddenly you're approached by an acquaintance who is demanding to know why he wasn't invited.

Sometimes we do things that are perfectly within our rights and for which we should not have to apologize. But the hurt or angry reactions of others can still leave us feeling awkward, guilty, and unhappy. You do not have to invite everyone you know to your party. Certainly, as discussed earlier in this chapter, it is not nice to invite the entire crowd except one person. But other than this situation, you should not feel compelled to hand out invitations to people just because they will find out about your party. Still, knowing that you are within your rights won't help much when you are confronted. You really have only two choices:

You can explain that the party is a small one and that you simply couldn't invite everyone. The next bigger party you throw, you'd be happy to invite him.

You can explain the party was to celebrate a particular event that clearly does not involve him, such as a big tennis win or a pre-dress-rehearsal shindig. (Obviously, you should only choose this option if it is true.)

Whatever you decide, try to remember you have done nothing wrong. The person who has confronted you, however, is doing something wrong *and* unfair. Still, she is doing it mostly from hurt and so it would be savvy to respond *sensitively*. Doing so will help both of you feel better.

Whether you intend to send invitations, give them out by hand, or offer them verbally, do remember one thing. The invitation should be extended at least two weeks in advance of the party. (For more formal affairs a month to six weeks in advance is wise.) That way you will have informed your guests of the party before they've had a chance to make other plans.

If you are sending an invitation, the following information should be included:

- Reason for or type of party (for example, a Birthday Dinner Party or a Valentine's Dessert Party)
- Date
- Name of person giving the party
- Place
- Time
- Dress (casual, semiformal, formal/black tie)
- Whether or not you need a response and how it may be done

This last item can be handled in any number of ways. If you write R.S.V.P., which is the abbreviation for the French *répondez s'il vous plaît*, and which in English means, "Please reply," people will know to get back to you. Sometimes the R.S.V.P. is followed by a date (for example, R.S.V.P. by October 5). You would include this in your invitations if the planning of your party depended on your knowing a specific head count in advance. Or, you might simply write "Regrets only" on your invitations. This would indicate you are giving a large, rather informal party (no sit-down meal!) and that you need only a general idea of whom to expect.

Store-bought invitations have a place for almost all of this information. No chance you'll forget to tell any of your guests something they need to know! But suppose you decide to make your invitations? Just make sure the paper you use is big enough to accommodate all the necessary particulars!

decide on the menu

Once you have decided on the kind of party you are throwing (for example, dinner or a snack and movie) and planned your budget, you will be able to plan a menu intelligently. Perhaps even more importantly, you will be able to do so in advance. No one likes to walk into a party and see their host or hostess running around in the kitchen as if the house were on fire, hastily throwing together bowls of this and trays of that. It makes guests feel as if they *have* to help—as if their presence at the party is just too much for the host or hostess. So, in the interest of allowing your menu and its presentation to reflect your party savvy, keep in mind the following suggestions.

• Pick foods most people like.
• Do whatever food shopping you can way ahead of time. Bags of chips, sodas, and ice cream will keep perfectly well until the party.
• Keep an eye out for any specials in the supermarket. The money you save could go toward some great decorations!
• Prepare as much of the food as possible well before the party begins. For example, if you are serving pasta, the sauce will keep a day or two ahead of time. All you'll have to worry about is the pasta.
• Make sure you know where the important serving pieces are in your home. If you're offering simple snacks, scout around the house for

nice bowls and check with your mother to find out if it's all right to use them. Rinse them out and put them in a convenient place. Fill them an hour before the party begins.

• If you have not included ice cubes in your budget (these can be bought in large plastic bags), then get busy days in advance! Start filling ice trays and dumping the cubes into freezer bags at regular intervals.

• Set the table hours in advance, whether it's a formal meal or a buffet. That way you'll have time to rearrange the look of things until you're satisfied.

clean up and set up

Surroundings are very important. If the house is messy or the basement hasn't been cleaned out in ages, get cracking! Do a little bit at a time the week before the party so that the job is not too overwhelming. If the party is supposed to be outside, then do a clean-up job there too! Is the grass cut back? Are the leaves off the lawn? Is the lawn furniture clean? Finally, be sure your home is prepared for guests in these particular ways.

• Create a space for coats and, in case it rains, a spot for wet boots and umbrellas.
• Be sure you have fresh hand towels, paper or cloth, to hang in the bathroom.
• Place a box of tissue and an extra roll of toilet paper in the bathroom.
• Make sure you have enough seating for everyone. If you are running short, borrow some bridge or lawn chairs from friendly neighbors. (If you're borrowing from several people, put their names on pieces of masking tape and affix them to the bottom of each chair.)
• If you're planning to give out favors, be sure you've chosen them thoughtfully and that they are nicely wrapped.
• Remove breakables. People can get careless at parties. They're so busy talking, looking around, and eating that accidents can easily happen.

decorate your party

Decorations can offer you an opportunity to display your sense of humor, be original, and perhaps even more importantly create a mood! In fact, if they are really imaginative, they can even serve as conversation icebreakers.

Decorations include everything from lighting and window trimmings to dishes, napkins, wall posters, and flowers. You can be as simple or as wild as you like! Here are some examples.

• For a Valentine's party, you might want to decorate the house with red cutout hearts and beautiful photographs of romantic places (clipped from magazines.) A red-and-white tablecloth and matching carnation centerpiece would create a very festive table.
• A "South of the Border" party could mean that you hang a few straw sombreros on the wall, use bright orange, pink, and blue paper tablecloths and napkins, and hang a big Mexican travel poster on your front door!

A creatively decorated room is a way of saying to your guests, "I love giving parties and I want you to have a good time." They will feel very relaxed and welcome.

the entertainment

Will you all gather around the TV to watch an exciting old movie or are you planning to have a dance or pool party?

If you plan on playing music at your party, what kind would you like it to be? Should it echo the theme (Mexican folk songs) or can it just be your favorites?

Whatever you decide, make sure you have enough space so that everyone can enjoy themselves. If you would like your guests to dance, make sure you've cleared a space that is large enough to accommodate everyone. If everyone is planning to gather around the TV, be sure you have enough chairs and pillows to go around so that everyone is comfortable. If you're simply planning to play music, make an effort to accommodate everyone's tastes. Not every person likes hard rock or rap. Why not put out a few jazz, soft rock, and even folk tapes? That way, as the mood of the party shifts (as it always does), the music can keep pace.

I would also suggest that no matter what the planned entertainment, you present people with another option. Suppose you're giving a swimming party, but a few guests don't really like the water? What if it turns out the TV movie you are watching is boring a few people? Make sure the Ping-Pong table downstairs is cleaned off. Perhaps you have a backgammon or chess set you can leave out. And of course there are always cards, magazines, or the dart board, which you might put in a conspicuous place.

One final note: Whatever your plans, it's always fun to add a surprise activity. For instance, if you're all watching a movie, at the conclusion why not hand out scorecards for your guests to rate the acting, script, beauty, and thrills, and then tally up!

giving a party: you're on!

As the host or hostess of a party it can be a wonderful feeling to watch one's friends have a terrific time. But you also have a great deal of *responsibility* in many areas. In fact, at times it can feel as if you were doing a very fancy tap dance in order to keep everything going just right. You want your friends to have a good time, but you need to follow your parents' rules. You'd like your guests to be relaxed, but you must always be aware that this is your family's home. It's important to make sure the refreshments continue looking appetizing throughout the party, yet you need to also make sure there are no people standing alone! There's so much to watch for, it's easy to lose track. Here's a checklist of things to attend to.

• As soon as your guests arrive, either take their coats or show them where they can be placed. Then direct them into the party room and invite them to enjoy some refreshments.

miserable

m
o
m
e
n
t

You have thrown a big party, and sud-denly one of your guests shows up at the door with liquor. A number of your guests flock toward the newcomer, happy to see she's brought "something real to drink."

It can be dreadfully uncomfortable lay-ing down rules with friends. They may feel you are being bossy or obnoxious or no fun or, worse, completely not "with it." But remember that whatever it is these friends *feel*, it doesn't make it right. Sometimes you just have to listen to yourself. Friends showing up at your door with alcohol is not right. It is illegal for minors to drink. Also, younger people tend to be quite inexperi-enced with liquor and thus consume way too much. It can make them ill and/or ter-ribly inappropriate in their behavior. It can also result in dangerous accidents. So what do you do? Gather up your courage, walk over to your guest, and say, "Look, I'm glad you could come, but alcohol is not allowed at this party. Let me put it away somewhere." If your guest insists you're being ridiculous, then keep your cool and say, "I don't think I am. If you have to drink this stuff, please do it someplace else. Not in my home." You haven't scolded her. You haven't played the part of her parent, informing her that liquor isn't good for her and that she's too young. You've simply made a statement about *your* party and how *you* want to run it. You have informed your guest she is free to make her own decisions—but so are you.

• Make introductions. This is especially important if the room is half empty (which it always is at the beginning of a party). Make sure everyone has someone to talk to. Bring up a subject two people who don't know each other very well might have in common. (See Chapter Two for savvy tips.)

• Check your refreshments. Is everything in place? Did you underes-timate the amount of soda people might drink? If so, put a few more bottles in the refrigerator or fill a pitcher with water and ice. Add more glasses or paper cups, if necessary.

• Circulate. Spend a little time with each guest so that each person will know you were looking forward to seeing him or her.

• Be aware of bad vibrations. If two friends have gotten into a loud disagreement, or if it seems that one person is being picked on, walk over and see if you can help resolve the problem. In other circumstances it might be none of your business. But this is your party, and anything that could destroy the good spirit in the room *is* your business.

• Watch out for noise levels. The last thing you need is angry neighbors calling to complain or guests who can't hear themselves talk. If the music is turned up too loud, walk over and turn down the volume. If people are doing too much shouting, quietly explain you don't want any trouble from the neighbors. Sometimes, telling friends how to behave can feel quite uncomfortable. But if their behavior is threatening to cause trouble for everyone else, then you do need to take control.

• If you notice that people are not being careful of their surroundings, lend a hand. If someone is repeatedly putting a glass down on a wood surface without using a napkin or coaster, simply walk over with one, slide it under the glass, and say, "Could you use this? I don't want anything to get stained."

• If you feel the party is a bit slow—people aren't talking or dancing much—then shake things up a bit! Suggest a word or picture game, or put on a favorite dance record and invite someone to join you on the "dance floor."

• As the party draws to a close, help your guests retrieve their things and accompany them to the front door. Tell them how nice it was to have them and that you hope they had a good time.

• If a few people seem to be dragging their heels about leaving, then begin cleaning up as you chat with them. One or two may leave immediately and a few friends may linger a while to help, but very soon you'll be on your own!

• Clean up in accordance with your parents' wishes. They may want everything back in order as soon as the party is over. If it's an evening party, they may expect you simply to clean up the kitchen directly after the party and save the rest for the morning. The point is, it's their house too. If you *respect* their rules, you're likely to have another party. (By the way, if you find any items left behind by guests, put them in a safe place. The owners will surely call.)

• Finally, put together a "party book." Memories are a lovely part of any party and this will provide you with a space to record specifics about the music, food, and entertainment. You can use an attractive cloth-covered book, or even something that resembles a school note-book. Include a copy of the invitation, photos of the group taken during the party with fun captions written underneath, recipes for food that went over well, bits of confetti if you used it, or even a list of the favorite music played. The next time you plan a party, pull out your book and you'll know what to do in an instant!

attending a party

Guests have so many surprises to look forward to at a party. Who will be there? What will everyone wear? What kind of food will be served? Whom will you meet? Certainly you can expect to have a great time. But just as a host or hostess has a role or job to fulfill, so does a guest. When attending a party, it is your *responsibility* to behave in a festive manner (even if you're not in the mood) and to go along with your host's or hostess's plans (no insisting on loud dance music during dinner!). Here's a guide to what you need to keep in mind from the moment the invitation is offered to the day after the party is over.

respond as requested to an invitation

Respond as quickly as you can to an invitation, and mark it on your calendar. That way your host or hostess will be able to plan for the correct number of people and you won't forget and make another date. Always respond in the manner requested on the invitation. If it says to call, then do so. If it says to write, and a printed response card is not included, then pick up a pen and begin.

Dear Mrs. Balter,

Thank you for inviting me to the surprise party for Jenna. I'm really looking forward to being there.

Sincerely,
Megan

It can be, however, a more sensitive task to turn down an invitation. A no can feel to some like a rejection. It is important to express your regrets in a way that your friend won't feel hurt and your sincere good wishes for a great party shine through.

Dear Joanna,

Thank you so much for the invitation to your party. I would have loved to come, but I'm going to be away. I'm sure the party is going to be terrific, though. I hope you'll tell me all about it when I get back.

Your friend,
Louie

Sometimes because of a family responsibility or tentative other plan, you may not know until a few days before the party if you can attend. If the party is a big one and not centered around an intimate meal, it is all right to ask your host or hostess if you can let him or her know at the last minute. However, if the party is a small one and knowing the head count in advance is clearly important to your friend, it would be better to simply tell him or her that because of some other plans you can't commit. Your friend may or may not say you can let him or her know a few days in advance. If he or she does, great. If not, don't be hurt. You were very thoughtful to recognize your friend's position. This kind of honesty and understanding between friends will only bring you closer.

A final suggestion: If you are unable to attend, a very nice way to express your regrets, aside from the note or call, is a contribution to the party. Dropping off a tray of brownies or a pretty basket filled with popcorn says "Even though I can't be there, I want you to have a great time."

find out what to wear

If you aren't sure of what to wear, ask your host or hostess. It can be very embarrassing to walk into a party in your favorite fancy outfit, only to find everyone is dressed in jogging suits! Even if the invitation seems clear, it's a good idea to check. A pool party certainly means a bathing suit. But it may also mean a change of clothes for dinnertime.

decide what to bring

It's always nice to ask in advance if there's anything you can bring. If your host or hostess says no, you might still make a few suggestions, saying something like, "Are you sure? How about some soda or a couple of bags of chips?" If the answer is still no, you might then elect to show up with something small but thoughtful, such as a box of special peanut-and-chocolate candies. When you arrive, say, "These are for you," thereby leaving it up to your host or hostess to use them or not for the party.

how to help

Once you've arrived, it would be nice to ask your host or hostess if you can help in any way. If he or she says yes, then go ahead and lend a hand. However, your friend may respond by saying, "Just enjoy the party. In fact, why don't you introduce yourself to . . ." In this case, don't take his or her casual suggestion too lightly. Remember, part of helping a host or hostess is to mingle, enjoy yourself, and contribute to the spirit of the party. Sometimes guests can help one another feel relaxed, and in so doing make things quite easy for the host or hostess!

During the course of the evening, you might notice that a piece of food has dropped to the floor or a water stain is forming on a surface. Pick up a napkin and do what you can to clean things up. It's a *respectful* way to behave in someone's home.

If the host or hostess is a good friend of yours and you notice that

m i s e r a b l e

o

m

e

n

t

The party you are giving is moving along splendidly. In fact, everyone is having such a good time, the noise level in one part of the room is way too loud. You've asked your friends to keep it down once, but there doesn't seem to be a change.

Walk over once more and say very nicely that you're glad they're having such a good time, but that you have to remind them again to keep it down. You don't want any trouble from neighbors, and your parents are getting annoyed. If a moment later the loud voices return, bring your friends their coats. Smile and good-humoredly say, "I just can't let you do this here. This is my home and I don't think it's fair that you're ignoring what I've asked. I might be forced to end the party and I don't want that to happen. Maybe you should all take a walk or something. When you calm down, come back."

the chips bowl is empty or that the soda is almost gone, quietly volunteer your help. If your friend asks you to refill the bowl or bring out more bottles, great! But if not, he or she will appreciate that you acted as a "scout."

get into the swing of things (or at least don't interrupt it!)

More than anything, hosts and hostesses want their guests to have a good time. Still, parties are not a free-for-all. If it's an early evening TV movie party, don't try to get everyone to play Ping-Pong. Sit quietly during the movie, offer to get others something to drink when you get up to fill your own glass, and generally be *respectful* of the entertainment. If it's a quiet dinner party, don't insist that you'd love to play a game of darts. To sum up, enjoy yourself, but within certain boundaries. If you want to jump around and shout a lot, wait for the next day's baseball game. The bottom line is *compromise*. You don't have to watch the movie, but that doesn't mean you should put on your own show.

taking your leave

First seek out your host or hostess and tell him or her what a nice time you have had. If you are leaving early, say a quiet good-bye to a few friends and then depart without much ado. If you were to make a big deal about your departure, other guests might think it was time for them to leave as well. On the other hand, if it's the end of the party, you can say a special thank-you to your host or hostess, and then say good-bye to each friend individually or "Good-bye everybody! This was great" to the crowd. If your friend's parents are around, say good-bye and thank you to them as well. Whatever you do, remember the times stated on the invitation. If it said 2:00 P.M. to 5:00 P.M., then don't stay past 5:00. Chances are, your friend and his or her family have other things to do.

writing thank-you notes

No later than a few days after the party, sit down and write a note expressing how much you enjoyed yourself. (If it's a close pal, you might just call the next morning.)

> Dear Elena,
>
> What a great party! The lasagna was delicious (what's the recipe?) and your friends from camp were a lot of fun—I can't believe we all finally got to meet one another! I had a great time.
>
> Your friend,
> Donna

Or, in the event that the party was given by an adult, you might want to offer a more formal thank-you.

> Dear Mrs. and Mrs. Bernard,
>
> I was so glad to be at Helen's engagement party. The flowers were beautiful, the food was delicious, and Helen looked so happy. I enjoyed myself very much.
>
> Sincerely,
> Fatima

m i s e r a b l e

o
m
e
n
t

You're at a party where you know almost no one. You've managed to introduce yourself to a few people, but after you get past "Hello. My name is Peter," you can't seem to start a good conversation. Everyone keeps excusing themselves, leaving you standing alone.

First of all, conversations take two people. It's not completely up to you to begin, continue, or end a conversation. So don't place the blame for a "going nowhere" conversation entirely on your shoulders. It is savvy, however, to realize that if one conversation opener isn't working, it's time to try another. Why not walk over to the music area, where stacks of tapes or records are probably standing? Flip through them, pick one out, turn to the person nearest you, and say, "This group is great. Don't you think so?" or "Who's in charge of the music here. I'd love to listen to this. I tried to get tickets to their last concert, but it was all sold out." Chances are a pleasant conversation will follow. Why? Because of what I have referred to earlier as "volleyballing." You've said something that another person can "volley" back. You've introduced a subject that is easy to discuss. Two people are needed to make a conversation work. But someone has to "serve" the ball. Why not let it be you?

Everyone loves to hear their party was a success. Whether you choose to use a pretty blank card or your personal stationery or simply the phone, do express your appreciation. Your host or hostess will appreciate your efforts more than you can imagine.

special parties, special tips

weddings

Weddings are usually very carefully planned events at which everyone plays a part. You, as the guest, are the celebrant. This means you have come to share in a very joyous occasion. The bride and groom and their families will want you to have a terrific time, but they will also expect you to go along with whatever traditional touches their wedding includes.

the receiving line

After the ceremony and directly before the reception the bride, groom, and their immediate families form a line to receive congratulations. Guests are expected to stand on line and wait patiently as each person ahead of them greets each member of the bridal party. Often guests may know only one or two people whom they are expected to congratulate. They must therefore not only offer congratulations, but also introduce themselves, explaining how they came to be at the event: "Congratulations. It was such a lovely ceremony. My name is Beverly. I've known Helen (the bride) for a long time. We lived down the street from each other." Or, "Congratulations. It's a pleasure to meet you. I'm Tom Egan. Mitchell (the groom) is my second cousin."

the reception

After you have walked through the receiving line, there will probably be a short period during which people nibble on light hors d'oeuvres and have drinks. If there is to be a seated dinner, you will probably notice a table filled with little place cards. Find the one with your name and notice the table number. When dinner is announced, find the table with that number and take a seat. As others approach your table, say hello and introduce yourself. Arranging table seating is a very difficult task for the hosts. They will try to sit everyone with someone they know. Still, there will likely be a number of people dining at your table whom you have never seen before. It is important to say hello and make some small talk. Possible topics are:

- How nice the ceremony was
- How beautiful the flowers look
- How you know the bride and groom

- How pretty the bride looks
- What a nice couple the bride and groom are

When your meal is served, don't ask if there is anything else. There isn't. The hosts have designed a particular menu with very specific items. You are not at a restaurant.

The first time the bride and groom enter the room together, usually to an announcement, everyone stands. A bit later, when the best man gets up to make a toast, you do not have to stand unless everyone else does. However, you should raise your glass (it doesn't matter what's in it) and clink your glass with everyone else's at the table, or simply hold it up and say, along with the other guests, "Hear! Hear!" or "Amen!" or "Mazel tov!"

As for contact with the bride and groom, feel free to approach either one when they are moving about the room. Once they are seated, however, let them be. Weddings are thrilling and exhausting. Be *sensitive* and understand they deserve a quiet moment to themselves.

Finally, don't walk off with the beautiful floral centerpiece. It belongs to the hosts! The only exception is if the bandleader announces that whoever finds the table number under their plate may take the centerpiece. This means the hosts want to offer the flowers as a surprise gift. Still, whether or not you have the flowers in hand, remember it is very important upon leaving to say good-bye and congratulations to not only the bride and groom, but also their parents. In many cases it is they who have arranged the party, so be sure to express how much you enjoyed yourself and how pretty everything looked.

bar mitzvahs and bas mitzvahs

A Bar Mitzvah celebration can seem quite like that of a wedding. Depending on how lavish the plans, there might be a receiving line, a cocktail hour, a dinner or a luncheon, and dancing. Since it is celebrating the passage into manhood or womanhood of a thirteen-year-old, the party might also include games and special entertainment for young people. One difference, however, is in the receiving line. Usually the rabbi or cantor will also stand with the family of the person being bar mitzvahed. When you greet him or her on the receiving line, it is not as critical to introduce yourself as it is to comment positively on the ceremony. Anything complimentary would be lovely. "I enjoyed the service very much" or "What a beautiful service. Thank you" are good examples.

dances

First of all, remember this: No matter how uncertain your dance steps, no matter how shy you feel, and no matter whom you are with, don't spend your time in the bathroom. It doesn't matter if you don't dance one dance. It matters if you hide. People socialize while they're getting refreshments, listening to the music, and simply standing around. A lot of this can be fun. Of course, there is an expectation that you will take at least one turn around the dance floor. But whether you plan to or not, here's a guide to trying it, or not, gracefully.

• If you see someone with whom you'd like to dance, walk over and say, "Would you like to dance?" Simple. This goes for boys and girls. But if you're a girl and you feel uncomfortable asking a boy to dance, there are variations that might feel more comfortable. If you're standing near a boy whom you like, you might say, "Oh, I love this music!" After swaying a bit to the beat, you might say to him, "Let's dance to this, okay? I can't stand still." That's quite informal and very natural.
• If someone you've asked to dance says no, try not to let it get you down. There are so many reasons a person might say no—many having nothing to do with you—it's useless trying to sort it out. He or she could be tired, shy, or in a bad mood. Just nod and move on.
• If you've asked someone to dance and he or she says, "I don't know. I don't dance very well," you have a choice. You can say, "I'll teach you" or "Neither do I, but let's try," or you can simply stand there and start talking. Chances are you've asked this person to dance because you like him or her. Take the opportunity to be friendly. Teaching someone how to dance or simply talking instead is a very savvy way to turn a dance invitation into an opportunity to enjoy someone's company.
• Sometimes you might see someone standing all on his or her own, looking rather lonely. The term "wallflower" is often used to describe that person. Don't let looks deceive you! There may be a lovely and spirited light glowing inside—even though he or she can't get away from that wall! Sometimes when people stand for too long in a corner,

o

m

e

n

t

You are at a dance with a very good friend. You keep getting asked to dance, but not your friend. You feel terrible leaving her by herself.

When one friend receives a lot of attention while another doesn't, it can be quite painful for both. But let's face it—it's worse for the one who is left behind. You cannot force anyone to ask your friend to dance, but you can probably arrange things so that she is not left alone. When you are through dancing, excuse yourself and then casually approach your friend, hook your arm through hers, and lead her over to a small group of people you might know. If she doesn't know them, make some introductions. As a result, four things might happen. One, she won't be left alone the next time you dance. Two, someone from the crowd might ask her to dance. Three, since your friend will be chatting with others, she will probably appear quite friendly. That might inspire someone to whisk her onto the dance floor! And four, there's always the possibility of a free-style group dance in which everyone standing together simply dances together!

they just can't walk away from it. They begin to feel and then look very unapproachable. Also sad. It is not your responsibility to ask someone you are uninterested in to dance. But it's always terrific to uncover something special in unexpected places. If you're curious, go with it! Walk over and ask this person to dance, or just start talking. You may discover something wonderful.

Parties take a lot of *know-how*. Whether you're the guest or the host or hostess, you each have a *responsibility* to contribute to the event. Enjoy yourself, but remember you're not the only one at the party who wants to have a good time!

SEVEN

and tonight, our special guest is . . .

*T*here's nothing like having or being a guest to enjoy a change in routine. If you are the visitor, it can be great fun to participate in the day-to-day activities of another family. If you are the host or hostess, it can be just as much fun to have an ordinary day at home feel quite different (which it always does) with the presence of someone new. Still, no matter what role you are playing—host or guest—and no matter how much fun it is, there is one *responsibility* everyone shares. And that is to be considerate.

The most important job of a host or hostess is to make sure a guest is comfortable. Making sure he or she knows the rules of your house, has fresh towels, enjoys what is being served for dinner, and has a comfortable place to sleep are examples of consideration. These actions say, "I want you to have a good time."

The most important role of a guest is to fit into his or her new surroundings and to have a good time. Willingly learning a new family card game, spending a minimum amount of time in a shared bathroom, and helping to set the table are examples of consideration. These actions say, "I like being here. Thanks for having me."

Whether you are a host or a guest, one thing is for sure. You are not alone. Let's explore how to make sure everyone involved feels comfortable, confident, and excited about a return visit!

how to be a good guest

As a guest, you will want to both fit in and feel comfortable. Some of this will be up to you and some won't. If your friend forgets to offer you something to drink when you arrive, or gives you a terribly flat pillow at nighttime, those things happen. There are, however, many things you can do for your own comfort that will probably suit your hosts (your friend and his or her family) just fine. After all, if you feel comfortable, you'll have a lovely time—and enjoying oneself is the best gift any guest can ever give a host.

bringing gifts

If would be a very nice gesture if you are a dinner or overnight guest to bring your friend's parents a small gift. A simple bouquet of flowers is always appreciated, as is a small potted plant or a sweetly scented candle. Of course, if the dinner is very informal and you are often invited, it isn't necessary to bring something each time. But an occasional small gift is a nice way of saying you do not take the lovely invitations for granted.

If you are a weekend guest, I believe it is important to bring along something small yet thoughtful. It needn't cost a lot of money, but it should be something "special." By this I mean something your friend's parents might not ordinarily buy for themselves but which they and perhaps the whole family might enjoy. Some suggestions:

- Homemade chocolate chip cookies (two dozen, at least)
- Two pretty mugs filled with jelly beans or peanuts
- Four to six napkin rings
- A small box of assorted scented bathroom soaps
- Two small guest towels
- A box of chocolates
- Two hand-dipped tapers
- Straw place mats (one for every family member)
- Fresh vegetables from your family garden
- A seasonal basket of fruit
- A Christmas tree ornament (if it's December)

social savvy

miserable

You accidentally break a pretty vase that belongs to your hosts.

The first thing to do is to apologize. Then carefully clean up the mess. Once this is done, ask about the item you have broken. If it can be replaced, despite any protests from your hosts, tell them you will do so. (You will have to discuss this with your parents, as it may involve borrowing some money.) If it is a precious family heirloom, offer to have it fixed at your expense (again with your parents' help.)

If the item cannot be replaced either because the store no longer carries it or because it is an heirloom, then do your best to select another vase. It won't replace the loss, but it will show your *respect* and sense of *responsibility.* And, of course, whether you plan to buy a new one or fix the old one, when you arrive back home, write a note of apology.

(By the way, if the accident happens at the beginning of the visit, try not to hang your head in shame for the next forty-eight hours. I realize that you will feel uncomfortable. But the truth is, you didn't mean for it to happen. Everyone knows that— including your hosts.)

If your parents were given a small gift that has remained unopened and that they are pefectly happy to part with, don't be shy! There are no rules that say you have to buy something. How much you spend on a gift or where you get it is not the point. That you are thoughtful enough to bring something tasteful and attractive *is* the thing that counts. (If someone is rude enough to ask you how much you spent or check labels to see where it was purchased, you can be sure of one thing: No matter what you brought, it would not have measured up.)

One final note: Do take the time, no matter what you choose, to wrap the gift with care. A pretty paper and matching ribbon will not only convey your appreciation but also help to make the present itself seem that much nicer.

attire

There are three things to keep in mind when planning what you will pack and how you will present yourself while visiting:

- Modesty
- Appropriate clothes for the occasion
- Neatness

I do believe that modesty is the best policy. Every family has a different attitude toward the way they walk about the house. Some wander around with only pajamas and nightgowns. Others insist on the addition of bathrobes. During the summer months, skimpy bathing suits may be quite acceptable in some homes while in others cover-ups are important. The best thing to do is to ask in advance. But if that's not possible or comfortable for you, then play it safe and bring along a robe.

If you're unsure of what you will be doing with your friend for the weekend, then ask. That way you will bring along the correct clothing. If dinner at a fancy restaurant is planned, you will want to pack dress clothes. If you will be playing tennis, then you will want to bring along your sport clothes. Also, some homes have mealtime rules. Perhaps people have to be showered and dressed before coming downstairs for breakfast. T-shirts may not be allowed at dinner. Jackets may be insisted upon Friday nights. Knowing this in advance will help both you and your hosts feel more comfortable.

Of course, no matter where you are and what you are doing, try to look neat and clean. Hair should be combed. Shirttails should be tucked in. Clothes should be ironed. And, of course, hands and face should be freshly washed.

Taking the time to look well groomed at someone's home is a way of expressing *respect*. It says, "I want to look nice in your home because you have a nice home."

packing savvy

What, you might say, does packing have to do with social savvy? The answer is this: Looking neat and well-dressed is a big part of being a welcome guest and neither thing can be accomplished if you don't pack right!

Here is a list of packing tips you should always keep in mind.

• Heavier items should be packed on the bottom. In this way things won't get crushed.

• Shoes need special attention so that they do not soil your clothes. First wipe off the bottoms with a damp cloth. Then place the shoes in a plastic or shoe bag, and since they are a heavy item, pack them at the bottom of the suitcase.

• It is a good idea to pack your brush, toothpaste, toothbrush, favorite shampoo, etc., in a toiletries bag. This is a special plastic-lined case that can help prevent accidental spills from ruining your clothes. *However*, do remember to tighten the tops of all your toiletries. A toiletries bag can still leak. (If you don't have one, you might use a simple plastic bag tightly wrapped with a twisty thing.)

• It is usually not necessary to bring your own towel for overnight stays. However, if it is a slumber party or if you are invited to a more

m i s e r a b l e

o m e n t

You are allergic to dogs and you didn't bring your medicine. Two cocker spaniels greet you at the door.

First of all, if you do have this problem, always try to remember to ask about pets in advance. Now, you have a few choices. If you are far from home and the medicine you need is sold without prescription, you could apologize for being unprepared and ask if someone might accompany you to the nearest drugstore. However, if you are close to home, you might instead call your parents to see if they could drop the medicine off, run back home yourself to pick it up, or explain the situation to your friend and, after checking with your parents, invite him back to your house for a sleepover date. The important thing to remember is that when it comes to your health, it is your *responsibility to yourself* that is most important. Don't be shy about taking care of your medical needs.

rustic setting such as a boat or campsite, you might offer to bring your own. That way your hosts do not have to burden themselves with an extra for you.

• If you are staying for the weekend, do ask your hosts what you will be doing, so that you are sure to bring the right things to wear. But don't arrive with a steamer trunk! Select your clothes at home, instead of bringing your wardrobe with you!

• If you are bringing some dressy clothes with you, pack them on top and upon arrival ask to be shown where you might hang them to avoid wrinkles. (You might actually want to carry more formal clothes on their hangers in a plastic or garment bag over your arm.)

upon arrival

Once you've arrived and properly greeted your hosts, ask (if they haven't already told you) where you might put your bag. They will likely direct you to the room where you will be sleeping. If there is time, you can begin unpacking. No need to rush—unless you're late and dinner is being served! If you have a few items that need to be hung up, ask your friend for some hangers. Before placing your clothes in the closet, you might say something like, "May I hang these here? I don't want to crush your things." This is a nice way of showing respect for his or her belongings. If your friend does not offer you any drawer space (he or she may not be able to!), then leave the rest of your clothes in the suitcase, shut it and place it in a corner. *Do not* place your toiletries bag in the bathroom unless it is your personal bath. It is unfair to clutter up counters with your paraphernalia. The people living in this house probably have enough of their own.

Once you have finished unpacking, it is time to be with your friend (and his or her family, should that be the situation). It would not be gracious to take a nap, even if the trip has been long. You can always turn in early. But you can, if no one offers, mention that you would like something to drink. It is true your hosts should look after you. But that doesn't mean you can't look after yourself too! Just do it nicely, remembering to say please and thank you, of course.

kitchen etiquette

Unless your hosts have a maid or butler who prepares and cleans up everything, it is important to participate. Take your friend's lead in this. If he or she begins to set the table, ask if you can help. If he or she is making a salad, you might create the dressing, set the table, or put out glasses and pour water. When the meal is over, do stand up and help to clear the table. Once you are in the kitchen, look at what's going on. Is your friend obviously expected to help clean up? If so, offer to do your small share. "How about I dry the dishes?" would be a nice thing to volunteer. So would "Where's a sponge? I could wipe off the table." The point is, you should make it clear you are perfectly happy to help. You should not, however, make yourself into the household servant. You are a guest. You might be expected to help, but you are certainly not expected to do heavy work. Leave the floor waxing, tile scrubbing, and burned-skillet scouring to your hosts!

Below are a few more thoughts for being a savvy guest when it comes to kitchen etiquette.

• If you use a glass, don't leave it on the counter. Wash it out yourself or put it in the dishwasher. Quietly do the same for your friend's dishes, especially if he or she is busy doing other things (like checking the newspaper for movie times).

• Don't open the refrigerator door unless you are invited to do so. If you'd like a piece of fruit to nibble on, simply tell your friend or host. There are many adults who are perfectly comfortable having guests look through their refrigerators. But there are many people who aren't. Once you figure out which of the two kinds of families you are visiting, act accordingly. Otherwise, your friend will feel quite uncomfortable.

• Don't drink the last drop, or eat the last crumb, of any food you might find in the house. Leave enough for someone else to have at least one satisfying portion. If, however, you have spotted something you desperately crave, ask your friend if anyone would mind if you helped yourself. If he or she says no, then enjoy!

Most people want two things from their bathroom. They want it clean, and they want it empty when they need it! At the beginning of this chapter I said the role of a guest is to fit in. When it comes to sharing bathrooms, fitting in is *all* important.

Usually people have particular bathroom schedules. Some like to bathe in the evenings. Some like to shower before breakfast. Still others after. These are not habits that are happily given up and so you will want to fit into your host's patterns. Just ask your friend to tell you the best time to use the shower. If he or she has not offered you any fresh towels, feel free to ask for one or two. Find out where you should hang them when they're wet and once you're in the bathroom, keep these points in mind.

• Bring your toiletries in their bag into the bathroom. When you're through, pack them up and bring them back to your room.
• If there are large bottles of shampoo or conditioner in the shower or bath, you may feel free to use a little. Do not, however, scrounge around in closed cupboards. If you forgot your shampoo, ask you friend if you can borrow some.
• After you are through brushing your hair and teeth, make sure the sink basin is clean. Rinse it out and if necessary use your damp wash-cloth or a tissue to get rid of any of your hair or spots of toothpaste.
• If you've used the bathtub, be sure to rinse it and clean it as de-

scribed above. If you've taken a shower, make sure none of your hair has collected on the drain.

• Usually you will be told to either hang your wet towel on the shower rod or a particular bar or toss it in the hamper. If you are supposed to hang it up, be sure to do so neatly.

• When you are through using the bath or shower, make sure the curtain is pulled neatly back into position and that it is tucked into the tub so water doesn't drip on the floor.

• Don't take too long! Cut corners wherever you can. Brush your teeth while you're waiting for the shower water to heat. Comb out your hair while you're waiting for the tub to drain. Blow-dry your hair in your room, not in front of the bathroom mirror.

the room where you sleep

Whether or not you have your own room, it is very important that you keep it neat. This includes *not* throwing your clothes all over, and promptly making your bed. A neat room makes it clear that you *respect* and appreciate your hosts' belongings.

If you are sharing a room, it is especially important to be *sensitive*

m i s e r a b l e

o
m
e

You accidentally left the light on all night in your friend's bathroom and now at the breakfast table his father asks, "Who left the light on last night? Doesn't anyone care about bills but me?"

n
t

Take a deep breath and remind yourself that everyone has done this a few times by accident. Then, fess up. In a serious tone of voice turn to your friend's father and

explain that you are sorry—it was the middle of the night and you must have been half asleep. You might add that you occasionally forget at home, too, and have been trying to break the habit. In all likelihood your friend's father will say you are forgiven and quickly change the subject. His intention was to stop the members of his family from running up the electric bill —not to embarrass a guest!

to your friend's territory. Carelessly throwing your things around may not only look bad, but also make him or her feel crowded. It is also wise to be flexible. If your friend goes to bed early and rises early, it is nice to do the same. That way you will have a lot of time together. Of course, if his or her habits are very different from yours, you can always—ask and if this is okay—go into another room to read or watch TV until you, too, are tired. In this way you will be *respecting* your friend's right to keep to his or her schedule, but also accepting your differences. This is a nice *compromise*. Just be sure not to stay up too late! Otherwise, he or she might spend the better part of the morning waiting for you to rise.

Below is a list of a few other things to keep in mind when it comes to your "guest" room.

• Make your bed neatly. A rumpled bed is not much better than an unmade one.
• If your friend wants to go to sleep, don't turn on the radio or television real low, thinking it won't bother him or her. It will. If your friend is used to having his or her own room, then he or she is used to silence.
• Your friend may like privacy when he or she gets dressed. Be *sensitive* to that and leave the room for a few moments.
• When your visit is over, ask your hosts if they want the bed stripped, and if so, fold the sheets and blanket in a neat pile.

saying good-bye

When it's time to leave, take one last look around your room to make sure you have left it neat, turn off the light, and carry your things to the front door. Thank everyone for a nice time. It is up to you to decide whether you would like to shake hands or kiss your friend on the cheek. Once you have arrived home, a thank-you note to your friend's parents is in order. For example:

> *Dear Mr. and Mrs. Morgan,*
> *Thank you so much for the lovely weekend. I had a very good*

time and especially enjoyed the delicious dinner Saturday eve-
ning. I hope to see you again soon.

Sincerely,
Adam

how to be a good host

Your most important role as a host or hostess is to help make your guest feel at home. A lot of this can be accomplished by thinking ahead. Your guide is a simple one: Consider what would make you most comfortable in someone else's house and then do those things for your guest. The truth is, no matter how close the friend—no matter how many times you say so-and-so is just like family—he or she isn't family. You know that and your friend knows that. He or she will never be as at ease in your home as you are. But you can go a long way toward making him or her "feel at home."

If you're organized, remain *sensitive* to your guests needs and *respectful* of your family's, and stand ready to *compromise*, then everyone should enjoy the experience.

before your guest arrives

It is a good idea to prepare in advance for your guest's arrival so that you do not take time away from your fun time together. Therefore, consider the list of suggestions below, which you can easily take care of during the week before the visit.

• Clean your room. Make sure there are no dust balls floating about and that you get rid of any clutter on your dresser or dressing table.
• Clean out your closet and leave a little room for your guest to hang a few items. If possible, do the same with your drawers, leaving half of one, if you can, for your guest's things.
• If you have twin or bunk beds, make up your guest's bed with fresh sheets. If you have some special sheets that you use only sometimes, ask your mom if your guest can enjoy them. A nicely made-up bed is *very* cozy.

• Your guest will need a set of towels. If you have your own bathroom, then hang an attractive set on a bar and when your guest arrives, point them out to him or her. However, if you share a bathroom, you should leave the towels neatly arranged on top of your guest's bed.

• There are lots of little items you might offer your guest that would make him or her feel well cared for and appreciated. I like to offer my guests a *guest basket*. This is a straw basket (which I might have saved from Easter) that I fill with a good recent magazine, a new toothbrush, a hand towel, a candy or two, some bath gel, and a fresh dainty bar of sweet-scented soap. It's my way of saying "When you come for a visit, I want you to feel special."

• Before your guest arrives, ask him or her what kinds of things he or she likes to eat and whether or not he or she is allergic to anything. When you go shopping with your mother, pick out a few items you know your friend will enjoy.

• Think about the trip your friend has made. If it has been a long one, he or she might want to wash up, have something to eat, or simply relax for an hour or two. You might like to have a light meal or a special cool drink available, and a few empty hours planned so that your friend knows he or she is not expected to start hopping!

when your guest arrives

Basically, when your guest arrives, you will want to do three things: Introduce him or her to other family members, help him or her get settled in, and acquaint him or her with how things work in your house so that he or she and the rest of your family can live together in harmony! With this in mind:

• Take your friend's coat and hang it up in the closet. Place his or her bag off to the side to be brought to your room later (by you!).

• Even if your father is out back mowing the lawn, bring your friend out to meet him.

• Ask your friend if he or she would like something to drink or eat or if he or she would rather get settled in first.

• Bring your friend up to your room and point out his or her bed, and the drawer or closet he or she can use.

• Show your friend which towels are his or hers and where he or she can hang them.

• Take this opportunity to tell your friend, if you haven't already, any "rules of the house." Must he or she wear a bathrobe? Is a jacket or dress required for dinner?

• Be sure to tell your friend to just ask if there's anything else he or she needs.

• If you can tell your friend is tired even though he or she is not admitting it, suggest he or she takes a rest. Tell your friend there are plenty of things you can do in the meantime. That way he or she won't feel uncomfortable taking you up on the offer.

• If your friend isn't too tired, take him or her on a tour of your house so that he or she doesn't feel lost.

• If your parents are relaxed about guests, let your friend know he or she is welcome to look in your refrigerator for a snack or drink anytime he or she likes.

Once your guest has settled in, it's time to get on with the business of having someone stay for a visit. Above all else, you need to stay open to his or her needs.

planning activities

Your guest has arrived and unpacked. It's time to get on with the reason you got together in the first place. To have fun! If you've made plans without discussing them first with your guest, you might want to make sure he or she will enjoy them. If your guest is not, for instance, interested in going to a basketball game or the horror flick playing in town, don't push it. You can always do these things another time. Instead, *compromise.* Discuss what kinds of things he or she would like to do, suggesting outings you, too, would enjoy. Perhaps he or she would like to go to the museum or would enjoy a bike ride. This is your guest's special time and his or her preferences should come before yours.

o

m

Your guest has arrived and the first thing that happens is that you get into a terrible argument. Now you wish she would go home.

e

n

t

Wishing is one thing. Doing something about it is another. If you and your guest have gotten off to a bad start, there are a number of things you can do. One, you could suggest that the two of you get something to eat, read, or watch TV. Stepping away from the argument by doing something that wouldn't require a lot of talking could give both of you time to calm down. Two, if this is a friend who is comfortable in your home, you might take a walk. This will give you an opportunity to collect yourself. Three, you could frankly say, "I feel awful. Let's not argue about this anymore. We're not getting anywhere. I like you and I want to have a good time. Let's discuss this when we're less angry."

Chances are one of these three options will lighten the spirit between you.

sitting down to eat with the family

It is difficult for some people when surrounded by a family they may not know well to ask for what they need or to join in on conversation. It is your job to make sure your friend has enough to eat, and that he or she does not feel left out. Watch his or her plate. If your friend seems to have eaten with gusto, quietly offer him or her a bit more. If he or she seems shy about saying yes, take some more yourself. Chances are, your friend will speak up then! If the conversation is centering on your older brother's day, or the family car's flat tire, then wait for a pause in the conversation and bring up something about your day with your friend. Above all, avoid having any of the typical arguments you easily slip into with your siblings. (Don't turn to your brother and tell him his hair looks like he just stuck his finger in a socket.) It is never pleasant for an outsider to witness a family squabble—no matter whom it is between or how many arguments he or she might experience in his or her own home. And, frankly, a tease that is offered in front of family members feels a lot different when it is offered in "public." Your brother could feel extremely embarrassed.

Note: If you find yourself witnessing an argument between your friend and his parents, leave the room. It would be less embarrassing for all of you. Familys can't always keep their troubles bottled up until they are alone. All you can do is stay out of it and let your friend know you're there if he wants to talk.

kitchen etiquette

It is perfectly all right, especially if your family does not have a maid, to expect your guest to help with the clean-up. But it is not okay to put him or her to work. Bringing in the dishes from the dining room, sponging off the table, and drying the dishes are all nice light chores —anything more involved than that and you are no longer treating him or her like a guest.

Perhaps the most important issue, though, is exactly how at home your guest should feel in your kitchen. Can he or she simply go into the refrigerator and cupboards on his or her own, or do your parents prefer that he or she ask first? Make the situation clear to your guest. But be sure, if your family is more formal, to check with your friend every so often to see if he or she needs anything to drink or eat. Your friend may be too shy to ask as often as he or she might like.

m i s e r a b l e
m o m e n t

You are at a friend's house and the two of you can hear his parents screaming at each other.

First and foremost, you need to recognize and be *sensitive* to how embarrassed your friend must feel. Commenting on the volume or content of the fight will only hurt him even more. "Gosh, they're loud!" or "My parents used to argue just like that before they got divorced" will only make matters worse. Instead, work toward removing yourselves from the scene. Suggest that the two of you take a walk or visit a friend. If it's too late at night, then try watching TV in another room and closing the door. If you find your friend is suddenly a bit short-tempered or sullen, give him some space. Don't feel hurt. You wouldn't be in a wonderful mood either if the tables were reversed.

social savvy

The bathroom is a private place. And not just when someone is in it! Medicines, over-the-counter drugs for various ailments, your mother's hair-color rinse, your father's dandruff shampoo, are all usually left in the bathroom. So be sure they are out of sight! It protects your family's privacy and your friend's comfort. Your friend is here to visit you—not to get acquainted with your family's medical and cosmetic needs!

If the bathroom is shared by several people, it is smart to tell your guest the best time to use it. As I said earlier, people usually use the bathroom at particular times. Don't ask your family members to change their habits. Rather, suggest to your guest some times when the bathroom is typically free. "My father likes to shower right before breakfast, around eight o'clock. Anytime after that is fine." (You might want to give up your own usual time for bathing, to accommodate your guest's preferences.)

As I'm sure you know, a nice hot shower or bath can make you lose track of time. If your guest is in the bathroom for a bit too long (more than twenty to thirty minutes) and your mother is wondering if he or she is taking swimming lessons, rap gently on the door and ask if everything is okay. If your guest replies yes, then simply ask when he or she will be out because someone else is waiting. He or she will get the hint. If when he or she emerges the bathroom is a bit messy, go in and clean it up yourself, so that your parents are not offended. Your guest will get that hint too!

the evenings

If you are staying home, you will want to help your guest fit into your family's plans. If everyone has decided to gather around the TV for a good movie in bathrobes and pajamas, fine. If your guest didn't bring a robe, then you will want to loan him or her one of yours. If you have only one, it would be very nice and *sensitive* to stay dressed, so that your guest does not feel uncomfortable. If you are offering a light snack, don't bring it out in a bag. Spill the chips or pretzels or raisins and nuts into a bowl and offer small napkins. A nice presentation can make even the most ordinary snack taste special.

If your friend is uninterested in the film your family is watching, then offer him or her a book or a magazine. Of course, if it's just the two of you and it's a film only you would like to see, your guest's desires ought to come first. *Compromise.* Watch something else both of you would enjoy.

When it comes time for bed and you're tired but your friend isn't, there's no need to force lights out on him or her. Again, offer your friend something to read and the use of the den or living room. Naturally, if your friend is the one who's tired, you should encourage him or her to get some sleep. Make use of another room until you, too, are ready for sleep. In this way you will be *respecting* each other's needs. (By the way, if your friend has to get up at a certain hour to catch a train or bus, set the alarm accordingly. If you miss an hour or two of sleep, that's a small price to pay for a fun visit and visitor!)

the morning

Be sure to let your friend know, in advance, how things work in your family. (Weekdays and weekends are bound to flow differently.) If you are a late sleeper and your friend is not, I would not insist that you get up at the crack of dawn just to keep him or her company. But pushing yourself to rise at a slightly earlier hour than usual would be very considerate. Still, whatever the day of his or her visit or the hour you awake, your friend will feel more comfortable knowing the following in advance:

• What the members of your family wear in the morning.
• If everyone makes their own breakfast. A guest should never have to *cook* his or her own breakfast. Cereal is fine. (If your friend wants eggs, get up and make some!)
• Whether or not everyone eats together.
• If he or she can go downstairs and watch TV before others rise.
• That he or she is welcome to have some juice before others rise.

When the visit is drawing to a close, your most important role as a host or hostess is to help your guest and keep him or her company to the very last minute. If your friend doesn't need your assistance packing, then sit down and chat with him as he is doing so. Offer to carry your friend's bag to the front door. Accompany him into the living room as he says good-bye to your parents. See your friend to the front door, bus stop, or train station and wait until the transportation arrives. If your friend is being picked up at your front door by family or friends, don't shut the door until they are driving off. And always remember to let your friend know, before you part, that you've had a terrific time—which brings me to my last point.

It's a funny thing about visiting, whether you are the guest or the host: Closing moments mean a lot. If the visit was great, but you neglect to bid someone a warm farewell, the other person will often feel confused and hurt—as if the visit wasn't so great after all. If the visit was tense, but you bid someone a warm farewell, acknowledging you weren't in a good mood or that the two of you got off to a rough start, then both of you will walk away feeling at ease and appreciated. So be sure to express yourself nicely. Those moments often set the tone for one of the nicest things about a visit—the memories.

3

social
savvy for
special
situations

EIGHT

money is a sensitive subject

*M*oney is a sensitive subject because people assign a lot of complicated meanings to it. Yes, the amount of money we have or earn says something about our financial worth. But it says nothing about our worth as people. And that is where we often become confused. Money is a sensitive subject because many people believe the amount they have equals their value as individuals. If they have a lot, they must be successful and important. If they have only a little, they must be failures or unimportant. But this is simply not true! Most politicians make less money than many business executives, and yet the decisions they make are tremendously important to lots more people! Some very wealthy people may be so unpleasant to be around that one could say they have failed miserably in their personal lives.

Of course, not all people attach their self-worth to money. They may in fact feel very proud of a particular profession even if the pay is not grand. Still, when it comes to money, many people are proud if they have it and ashamed if they don't.

How sad!

You can see why money is such a sensitive matter. When the subject comes up, many people feel as if they are being judged—as if their worth as a person were being questioned. If you feel this way, or you know anyone who has these feelings, then you need to read this chapter *very* carefully.

It's nice to have money. I would never deny that. It can make a lot of things easier. But it cannot buy true friendship, happiness, or love. Only you as a worthwhile and full person can find those things.

Every family has a different attitude toward money. Yours included. There are many reasons for this. It may have to do with how much money your parents had while growing up and how their parents handled their finances. Other influences might be how much money they now have, how concerned they are about the future, and, most important, their specific ideas about how to teach *you* the value of money. Still, no matter how your parents handle money, it is important that you *respect* their "way." Most people work hard for their money. Until you do so as well, it may be difficult to understand why it can't be parted with more easily. But once you begin to earn a living and pay bills, you will see why.

Before I go on to the specific issues of how you handle money with your family, I would like to stress one thing. Money is not just a sensitive subject out in the world. It's a sensitive matter at home too. Sensitive and private. Your parents want to feel they are making enough to give you everything you need. It may hurt them if they feel they cannot do that. They may want to keep their finances private because they want to protect you from worry or keep you from becoming spoiled, or simply because they feel it's none of your business! Also, money can cause unnecessary competition within a family. Your younger sister may feel your parents are more generous with you than

---

class quote

"Miss Judith," a young man said grimly, "my grandfather always gives me a few dollars when I see him and asks me not to tell my parents. I feel funny about that." I smiled knowingly. "Your grandparents give you money because it's their way of saying 'We want you to have something that's just between us.' That's a lovely gesture, but not one you can hide from your parents. After all, suddenly you have cash to spend! So tell your parents, and ask that they say nothing. They probably won't, because it would deprive your grandparents of the pleasure of giving."

---

her. You may feel that you need the same size allowance as your slightly older brother. As you can see, there's plenty of opportunity for money to become a sensitive issue at home! Certainly some amount of discussion concerning money is inevitable. But try not to let it get in the way of your relationship with your family. The truth is, sometimes the family is your greatest source of strength. Emotional strength, that is—not financial. If there is a good deal of money, then count yourself lucky. You won't have to worry if an important need arises. But even if you don't have a lot of money, but do have a family that is supportive and happy, you have all the luck you need.

how to ask for or negotiate an allowance

When it comes time to ask for or negotiate an allowance, the first question you need to ask yourself is, What for? Figure out what you need—such as money for snacks, lunch, transportation, movies, or extra clothes—over the course of perhaps a month. Be reasonable, of course. Estimate modest snacks. Realize you don't need to see a movie every week. Don't plan on replacing your entire wardrobe, and figure on walking at least to some places. Once you determine how much you need and for what reasons, then it is time to approach your parents. It might be helpful to do so with a piece of paper upon which you have worked out your budget. It might look something like this:

Transportation to and from school	$_____
After-school snacks	_____
Movies	_____
Clothes	_____
Drugstore items	_____
School supplies	_____
Weekend entertainment (food, transportation, sport fees, etc.)	_____
Extras	_____

Whatever you do, don't, in an effort to come in with a low figure, leave something out of your budget. In the end someone is going to "pay" for your error!

Sit down with your parents at a time when all of you can concentrate, and explain what your needs are. Show them the budget you have composed and discuss the entries. Answer their questions calmly and without getting upset, even if they say things like, "I don't think you need that much for clothes" or "You don't need to go to the pizza shop for a snack. Take some fruit from home." Your parents know how easy it is to go through money. The sum you are proposing may seem fine to you, but they may be anticipating you will use it up faster than you think. Also, don't forget this is *their* money for which you are asking! Stand ready to *compromise*. They may want you to cut down on your budget for entertainment. Or, they may agree to your allowance but request in return that once a month you clean out the garage and wash the car. Listen to their suggestions and points, and, above all:

- *Don't* tell them what your best friend is getting.
- *Don't* accuse them of being cheap.
- *Don't* run up to your room when they don't agree with every item on your list.

If you are reasonable and open to their views, chances are the three of you will reach an agreement quickly. And do stick to your budget! If you repeatedly come back to them saying, "Well, I don't know what happened! It just didn't last!" your parents may decide to end your confusion by ending your allowance!

the no-allowance route

Some parents do not believe in allowances. They prefer to simply give their children money as it is needed. Of course, everything is discussed, but there is no formal day of the week in which money is handed over, or even any specific budget. Again, this is your parents' choice. But it is your *responsibility* to control the amounts for which you ask. It can be tempting with this sort of arrangement to just keep asking. It is easy to lose track of what is actually being handed to you and even to feel annoyed because last week you got what you wanted but this week you did not. With no formal budget the picture *can* become confused. It is particularly important here to keep track of what you are spending and to carefully consider each request you make. At first glance it would seem that having a budget is really tough. After all, there's something in black and white that you must follow. But not having a firm budget is much trickier! You have to take the time to carefully consider the importance of each item, whether it's travel expenses, sports equipment, drugstore items, games, or anything else. Now it's not just a question of "Can I afford it?" but also, "Is it okay to ask Mom or Dad for more money?" Remembering to think before you ask is a big *responsibility*.

asking for a loan

Suppose you and your friends are planning a camping trip, but you need a new sleeping bag. Unfortunately, you don't have the money to buy one right now. You would like a loan from your parents. What's the best way to get one?

• Explain why you need the loan.
• Suggest ways you might pay them back, such as by subtracting a little from your allowance each week, doing extra chores around the house for a certain period of time, taking on small jobs for neighbors, or a bit of all three.
• Stick to your agreement. Let them see that once you strike a deal, you see it through.

The problem with family loans is that agreements are often sloppily treated. After all, it's not as if your mother or father would stop "liking you" or ask you to leave if you didn't pay them back on schedule. But that's the wrong way to look at it. A loan is a favor. Your parents give it to you because they love and trust you. Paying it back is a sign of your good feelings and *respect* for them. Failing to do so will only make you look irresponsible and make them feel disappointed. Next time you want a loan it will not be forthcoming. So, keep the following in mind:

- *Don't* ask for the loan saying, "Bill's dad lent him money!"
- *Don't*, upon your parents' indecision, say, "You can afford it!"
- *Don't*, after the first few payments, conveniently "forget" the rest.
- *Don't* say to your parents, "Can I return the rest of the money next year?"

Above all else, remember that a loan means you are borrowing. Borrowing means that you have something you must return. Keep your end of the bargain and you will find that you've gotten something you can keep forever—your parents' *respect* and trust.

when you just need extra

You're on the tennis team and your racket needs new strings. You're planning to go to the beach for the first hot day of the summer and you need to buy an umbrella to keep out of the sun. A teacher is retiring and everyone in the class is supposed to contribute something to his or her gift.

Every once in a while you may find that you need some extra money. It isn't for something insignificant like a new sweater to go with your new pants, or that great new tape by your favorite rock band. Rather, this is for something quite important or necessary. You would prefer that you could go to your parents without it being a loan. But of course your parents may be either unwilling or actually unable to simply hand you extra cash. Since you may not know how easy or difficult it would be for your parents to help out, here is a good way to approach the subject.

- Tell them what you need and why.
- If they hesitate, offer to do some chore around the house, such as cleaning out the attic, doing the wash, raking leaves, or weeding the garden.
- If your parents are obviously uncomfortable handing you any money, then suggest that you will pay them back.

No matter what the issue—your allowance, a loan, or extra money —the most important thing to keep in mind is that your parents' money is theirs! That they are willing and able to give you some so that you can move about your life more comfortably is your good fortune. People in families tend to take advantage of one another because they know the love will always be there. But much earlier in this book we discussed the idea of not taking advantage of your family. Well, this goes for money too. If you *respect* what your parents have, they are far more likely to understand what you need.

money and you

You may not feel self-conscious about your money. The fact that you have a lot or very little may have little effect upon you. You're not disappointed, you're not envious, and you're not prideful. It simply is the way it is.

But that's your business.

m i s e r a b l e

m o m e n t

Your family has a lot of money and you have a very sizable allowance. Most of your friends do not. You would like to buy an expensive sweater you have been admiring for a while and though you can afford it you would be embarrassed to wear it.

You can't hide from the facts. If you have money, you have money. Certainly your friends must be aware that your family is well-off. Chances are your house is lovely or the family car is expensive or you vacation in special places or you have always had extra cash around to spend on fun things. The problem is not that you have a lot of money or that you spend it on nice things. The problem is how to have it and spend it without hurting anyone else.

If you buy and wear that sweater, no one will be surprised. One friend may admire it openly; another, a bit jealous, may say nothing. But neither friend will be hurt if you put it on, look nice, and let it go at that. Therefore, don't, because of your discomfort, draw undo attention to the state of your finances. "I can't believe I bought this. I really shouldn't have. It was so expensive" may sound nice to you. But to your friends it would sound as if you were bragging and lying about your wallet. Don't do that. It's not worth the "price."

Just because you wouldn't mind discussing how much you have or how much the things you own cost, doesn't mean anyone else would be happy or comfortable listening to the details. This is largely because when people start talking about their money, others start thinking about their own. Silent comparisons are drawn. Envy may grow. Embarrassment may blossom. Discomfort may result.

Money is private business. You can still tell people about where you've been, things you've bought, dreams you have, your parents' successes or failures, without bragging or complaining about money. But you have to do so with *sensitivity*. Here's how.

• *Don't say*, "I'm excited. My father's taking the whole family to this really ritzy ski lodge. It's super expensive and plush!"
• *Do say*, "I'm so excited. My whole family is going on a ski vacation! The lodge sounds great!"
• *Don't say*, "I just got the most beautiful cashmere sweater. I took one look at the price and nearly died! But who cares?"
• *Do say*, "I just bought the prettiest sweater. I can't wait to wear it!"
• *Don't say*, "I wish I were rich like you and had such a big room all to myself. Mine is so small, because we're broke."
• *Do say*, "What a nice room! I'd love to have one this size, though mine is pretty cozy anyway."
• *Don't say*, "My father just got an important new job. He's going to be making so much money!"
• *Do say*, "We're really proud of my father. He just landed a great job."
• *Don't say*, "My mother was just laid off. We're *not* going to have any money now, so I probably can't go anywhere. Oh, well."
• *Do say*, "My mother has to find a new job, so things are going to be a little tight for a while. I'm going to have to watch what I spend."

money and friends

When it comes to friends and money, I have but one rule. And it is the following:

don't ask questions!

Your friends and their money is a private matter. They are entitled to keep how much they or their families have to themselves. Again, money is an emotional, *sensitive* subject. Everyone reacts differently. If a friend has very little, he or she may feel embarrassed or totally unaffected by it. If your friend has a tremendous amount of money, he or she may feel uncomfortable or proud. If your friend's parents lavish him or her with money, he or she may feel irresponsible, embarrassed, or just plain happy. Also, any one person may feel different ways, depending on to whom he or she is talking. The best advice, therefore, is to stay away from questions that get at the financial well-being of your friends and their family. For example:

- *Don't* ask if your friend's father makes a lot of money.
- *Don't* ask if your friend can afford an expensive restaurant.
- *Don't* ask why your friend isn't buying something new for the big party.

m i s e r a b l e

o

m

e

n

t

Your friends want you to go ice-skating Saturday afternoon, but you've just taken a job at the local candy and magazine store. You feel very embarrassed because they don't need to work for pocket money.

Your first impulse might be to make up an excuse, such as "Well, I promised my mother I'd help her clean out the closets." But what's the point of that? Since this is going to be a regular job, your friends will have to know sooner or later. Besides, what is it exactly you're embarrassed about? That your parents can't or won't give you the same money their parents give them? What about feeling proud that you had the energy, drive, and *know-how* to go out and find a job? How adult of you! Certainly you don't need to explain your job in a depressing or "woe is me" fashion. "My parents can't afford much, so I have to work" is not necessary. A simple "I wanted to make some extra money so I could buy myself extra things" is truthful, positive, and very impressive. After all, you have taken matters into your own hands. That is very savvy.

- *Don't* ask how much your friend's new purchase cost.
- *Don't* ask why your friend's parents haven't bought a VCR.

It's clear, of course, why you shouldn't ask about a parent's salary. It's private—or rather, it's none of your business. Asking what your friend can afford or why his or her family seems to hang on to old things is less obvious but *very insensitive*. What you are really asking is, "What gives? Don't you have the money?" *So,*

- If you want to know what your friend's father does for a living, then ask. That will tell you a lot more about who this man is than knowing what he makes.
- If you want to know if your first choice of restaurant is too expensive for your friend, give him or her three options: the one that costs a lot, one in the medium range, and the least-expensive choice. If your friend opts for the least-expensive restaurant, you'll have your answer without embarrassing him or her.
- If you notice your friend isn't buying anything new to wear to a party, ask if he or she would like to borrow something of yours. If your friend is pleased with an outfit he or she already has, the answer will be no. If your friend does want to wear something new, he or she will probably jump at the chance. In this way you will have given your friend a lift and saved both of you from an embarrassing moment.
- If your friend's new coat is beautiful and you want to buy the same one in a different color, ask where he or she got it. Go to the store and look at the price there. In other words, it's none of your business how much your friend paid for the coat. If it was very little, your friend may feel embarrassed that he or she couldn't spend more, and if it was a lot your friend may be too embarrassed to tell you—perhaps you won't be able to afford it. The important thing is that you tell your friend you like it! That will make him or her feel very good.
- If you're curious about why your friend's father drives an old car, don't ask why. That's like saying, "Can't you afford a new one?" In fact, don't say anything. For one thing, different people have different priorities. Saving for camp or college or old age may be more urgent

m i s e r a b l e

o m e n t

You are dying to go to a concert with your friend. The trouble is, you can afford the ticket but she can't.

You have a few choices. You can, if you have enough money, treat her, saying it's an advance birthday present. Or, you can lend her the money. Here it gets a little trickier. It's tough "doing business" with friends. The cleanest way to do this is to work out a date by which she will pay you back. That way your expectations and her *responsibility* will be clear. Or, finally, if you don't have enough money to either treat or lend, you can plan to go with someone else. This may feel cruel to you, but if you have saved the money from a job or an allowance, then you do have a right to enjoy it. Who knows? Perhaps your friend turned down a job because she wasn't in the mood. Maybe she spent her allowance on some unnecessary things and so now she's stuck. The point is, it doesn't make you a bad friend to fulfill your own wishes, even though your friend can't satisfy her own.

than a new car. It is not for you to question such choices. Also, cars, to many people, are status symbols. Some folks feel great if they have fancy wheels and drab if they don't. If your friend feels unhappy about the car, you will only make it worse. Of course, if you think the car is neat looking or in great shape for its year or very comfortable, then go ahead and say so. Some people get a kick out of hanging on to things forever and are very pleased when others notice!

It is human nature to wonder sometimes how much money people have. You will be curious about your friend's circumstances and he or she will be curious about yours. But that doesn't mean either one of you has to talk about it. The important thing is to know that money can't make a friendship. It can, however, break one. How much or how little each of you has won't cause the problem. But being insensitive to the differences between you will.

It sounds simple. You need money, so you look for a job. You find one. You begin working and at the end of the week you collect your pay. Smooth as can be. Right?

Not so fast! How much money will you earn? Can you influence how much you will be paid? What if your employer forgets to pay you or complains about your work? How do you ask for a raise?

Earning money can be very rewarding—especially if you have some financial savvy. So make it your "business" to know how! From baby-sitting to raking leaves to packing groceries, many of the same rules apply. *Responsibility* to both yourself and your employer is key.

negotiating your salary

Some jobs come with a set salary. A notice posted in the window of the grocery store or local candy shop may state the name of the job and the wages. In that case, there isn't much to negotiate. (When you get older, you will discover that a salary suggested by a possible new employer *can* be negotiated. But when you're younger and the job is simple and straightforward, the salary is usually firm.)

However, if you are seeking work on your own, such as baby-sitting, lawn mowing, leaf raking, window washing, fence painting, or even dog walking, *you* can influence how much you make. Sure, you can't force someone to pay what you would like. But you can—nicely, politely, and firmly—request what you think you deserve. And while you may not get it exactly, you might come awfully close if you:

- Know why you charge what you do
- Stick to your beliefs
- Stay polite and *respectful*
- Do what you say you can do

Let's take a look at a sample conversation to see how this works. Mrs. Mann has called and wants to know if Carol can baby-sit for her two-year-old son Saturday night.

Mrs. Mann: Carol, are you available Saturday night? My husband and I are going out and we need a baby-sitter.

Carol: I am. Do you need me for both children?

Mrs. Mann: No. Alex is sleeping at his friend's house. Tell me, dear, how much do you charge?"

Carol: Three dollars and fifty cents an hour.

Mrs. Mann: Oh. Actually, I usually pay sitters three dollars when it's just the baby.

Carol: I have been getting three dollars and fifty cents all season. I'd love to baby-sit for you. Jason is adorable. But I don't want to lower the fee. I have a lot of experience baby-sitting.

Mrs. Mann: Well, all right then. I guess it will be three dollars and fifty cents. You drive a hard bargain! Can you come at seven o'clock?

Carol: Absolutely.

Mrs. Mann: Thank you. See you then.

Carol: Thank you for calling. Bye-bye.

Now, let's consider what happened here. Mrs. Mann wanted Carol to do a job for her. Carol was available, but before she stated her price, she asked exactly what the job would entail. Once she established the nature of the job, she then stated her fee. Mrs. Mann, as was her right, wanted to pay a bit less. Carol felt that she deserved more and explained why. She also said something truthful yet flattering, hoping to show her sincerity. Mrs. Mann, realizing that Carol was not being unreasonable, agreed to pay Carol's price.

Let's try another situation. Billy wants to make a little pocket money. It's the fall, and he figures he can rake the leaves on his neighbors' lawns. He rings Mr. Snell's door.

Mr. Snell: Yes, Billy?

Billy: I was wondering if you'd like me to rake your leaves on the front and back lawns every Saturday morning? I'd bag them too.

social savvy

Mr. Snell: Hmmmm. It does take up a lot of my time. What are you charging?

Billy: Fifteen dollars for the morning.

Mr. Snell: Well, all right. But would you throw in the patio over on the side there? That old tree dumps a lot this time of year.

Billy: I'd be happy to do it, Mr. Snell, but that will take me a lot longer. I'd have to charge you for it.

Mr. Snell: How much?

Billy: Well, it's about a third of the space I was going to rake, so another five dollars. Is that all right?

m i s e r a b l e o m e n t

Two weeks ago Mrs. Ward asked you to baby-sit on a Saturday night. But now the day has arrived and she's just told you she and her husband have changed their mind. They're not going out after all. You are terribly upset because you were counting on the money and you turned down two baby-sitting offers.

The truth is, some people, however unintentionally, don't play fair. Mrs. Ward should offer to pay you a few hours of your baby-sitting fee. Baby-sitting is like running your own business. If you block out time, turning down other offers, you should be paid for that time whether or not your services are used.

Now that you are clear about your rights in this situation, let's look at your choices. You can hint to Mrs. Ward that you are in a bad position by saying, "Oh, I'm disappointed. I turned down another baby-sitting job just yesterday." If she doesn't take the hint, then you can decide not to baby-sit for her again. If you would rather not comment in this fashion, then the next time she calls, you might want to say you'd like to baby-sit but that if she's going to cancel, you need to know a few days in advance so that you can get another job. If she says this isn't possible, then you might choose to turn the job down, saying that if she hasn't found anyone by Saturday morning, and you're still free, you'd be happy to work that night. In essence what you would be doing is treating her as informally as she treats you. This isn't rude or inconsiderate. You are simply protecting yourself in a very honest manner.

Mr. Snell: Okay. But only if you bag those leaves, too, and drag them down to the corner so they can be picked up by the town truck. A deal?

Billy: You got it!

Okay, what happened here? Billy stated a price for a particular job. Mr. Snell thought it was okay, but he wanted Billy to throw in something big. The patio. Billy said no, explaining why but also making it clear he'd like to do the job if he was paid fairly. Mr. Snell heard him and offered a *compromise*. He wanted Billy to drag all the bags down to the corner. Billy felt that was a fair request, and so he agreed.

What did both Carol and Billy do successfully in both conversations? They were clear about the jobs at hand and how well they would perform. They stuck to their positions. And in both cases they were *respectful* and pleasant to the people with whom they were speaking.

negotiating a raise

Just as your salary requests depend on the nature of the job (whether you are being placed on a payroll or working independently), so does asking for a raise.

If you are on staff for at least six months and you've been working hard, you might decide you deserve a little more money. This is your right. However, don't expect your boss will agree it's time for a raise. The fact that you work hard is expected. Six months may not seem long enough to warrant a raise. None of this should stop you from asking, of course. But if he or she does say no, I wouldn't advise walking out. Here's some advice to stack the cards of a raise in your favor.

• Ask your boss when a good time to speak with him or her alone might be.

• Once you are alone, begin by telling your boss that you are glad you have the job.

• Tell your boss in a very straightforward manner that you want to discuss a raise with him or her.

• Explain why you think you deserve a raise. Speak only about your accomplishments on the job, not your personal needs. "I'm trying to save up for a camping trip" is none of your boss's concern.

• If your boss agrees to a raise, great. But don't ask how much. Simply say thank you and leave. You'll find out soon enough.

• If your boss tells you he or she has to think about it, say thank you and leave. If you hear nothing more in about two weeks' time, bring it up once more.

• If your boss says no, because the company cannot afford it and raises are usually given after someone's been working there a year, say thank you for his or her time and go back to work. If you are terribly angry and think you deserve more, then look for another job. But don't quit until you find one. That's a bad habit to get into. You'd be letting your pride put quite a dent in your wallet. (Naturally, if you are being mistreated, you should quit. But a raise refusal in most instances is more a difference of opinion.)

m i s e r a b l e

o m e n t

You've finished raking the leaves for Mrs. York. She's thanked you, but it's clear she's also forgotten to pay you.

It may surprise you to learn this happens a lot! If it's clear your "client" has forgotten to pay, first ask if the job was done to her satisfaction. If it wasn't and her request is reasonable (the lawn bags aren't tied), go back and finish the job properly. Then come back to the door and continue as you would have if she'd said the job was done beautifully. Smile at her politely and say, "I've finished the job. Would you like to take a look before you pay me?" It's not subtle, but it is honest, polite, and reasonable.

Now let's look at the situation in which you raise your own fees. Last spring you charged only $2.50 for baby-sitting. But this fall you feel you deserve more. How do you handle this smoothly with your "clients"?

• First of all, decide what you would like to charge, keeping in mind what other sitters get, what you deserve, and the simple truth that most people will accept only a small raise in fees. A sizable leap will send them in another direction. (A sitter used frequently by a friend of mine came back from the summer break and told my friend she'd be happy to sit but was earning more money now. My friend, used to paying $3.00 an hour, said fine, what would her fee be now? The sitter replied, $5.50. My friend promptly told her she would no longer be using her services.)

• When your client calls to see if now that you're back from camp you would baby-sit for her daughter, tell her right then and there that you are now charging $3.50. Don't wait until you show up that evening when she no longer has time to find another sitter. She would feel tricked.

• If your client says something like, "Isn't your fee a little steep?" explain why you think it's fair. Again, don't bring in your personal needs. It's not her business whether or not you are saving for a new tennis racket. Concentrate on the fact that you're older, more experienced, and very reliable.

• If she still insists it's too much, then politely say something like, "I'm sorry we don't agree. I would very much have liked to baby-sit for you, but I can't." If you know your price is fair, you will certainly find other jobs. (You might also invite her to call again if she can't find anyone else. This is called "leaving the door open." And don't worry —if she does call, it will be understood that you expect the new fee.)

you, money, and the rest of the world

I'm sure you've heard over and over that you should be grateful for what you have—that there are people out there who are in poor health, have no place to live, nothing to eat, and nothing to wear. And I'm equally sure that while you know that must be perfectly awful, it seems worlds away—that somehow *those* people with *those* problems have nothing to do with you.

Well, in a way you're right, and in a way you're wrong. Your friends, your home, and the places you go probably do reflect your own special, and in many ways privileged, world. And it is the details of this nice life, quite understandably, that concern you the most.

But, now, take a closer look. There are most certainly reminders in your world that there is another kind of life out there that some people are living. On your planet. In your country. In your town.

The drugstore might have a slotted-coin counter display for you to contribute something to a particular illness. Your school might have a canned goods drive for people on welfare. At Christmastime you might see fliers in the grocery store telling you where to bring your old winter coats that are no longer being used. And, of course, there are the homeless people in this country who are everywhere.

The point is, while you may not have a disease that needs a cure, others do. While you may have plenty of food in your kitchen cabinets, clothes in your closets, and a warm room in your own house or apartment, others don't. These people may not be in your life, but they live in your world. And while it is neither your obligation nor appropriate to give these people your money, it is your *responsibility* to care—and to translate that care into some action. If you can contribute some small amount of money, of course that's helpful. But there are other things you can do as well.

• Organize a bake-off on your street or at your school for a charity.
• If during holiday time you see a giant box that says "Any shoes would be appreciated" displayed in a public place, go home, clean out your closet, and bring back the pairs you no longer wear. Tell your friends and start a trend.
• Offer to stuff envelopes at the local headquarters for a particular charity. Stand in front of a local grocery store and distribute fliers.

Chances are at your age you are not in a position to give much money to important causes. But if you can do something to bring an important cause to the attention of someone who can help financially, you will have done something wonderful.

when you are directly approached for money

This country has a homeless population that is unfortunately growing. Some people who have no homes are alcoholics or drug addicts. Others have severe psychological problems that make it difficult for them to function productively in the world. Still others have simply fallen on very tough times and are ashamed or angry about their predicament. One thing they all have in common, however, is a kind of desperation.

Sometimes, in their desperation they might stop you and ask for money. This can be heartbreaking. Also frightening. You might even feel you are being threatened. Looking into the face of an unhappy, frustrated, or drugged person is a disturbing experience. So, what do you do?

I wouldn't advise you to stop and search for money in your pockets. Even if the person looks innocent, he or she may not be. Not everyone who presents themselves as having fallen on hard times is simply that. He or she may be, for instance, a pickpocket. The truth is, you may be too young to tell the difference. (Actually, a lot of adults could be fooled as well!) Simply murmur "I'm sorry," and keep walking. Once home, you might investigate either by phone or through the local paper where you might do some charity work. Food and clothing drives always need help!

The world isn't fair. Who knows why you were born into a situation that is secure while others were not? But just because the life of the homeless person is not your life, it does not mean that his or her problem should be ignored. It is your *responsibility* to be aware—not to shut out all unattractive aspects of the world because it seems they have nothing to do with you. They *do* have to do with you. And it is up to you to find a way to give in a manner that suits your circumstances.

on a happier ''note''!

In many cities and towns across the country, we are entertained on the streets by musicians and artists. Guitar players, flutists, violinists, sidewalk chalk artists, and caricaturists often display their talents out in the open. But that's not the only thing open. So are their pockets! Guitarists may leave their cases open. Artists may put hats on the ground bottom-side-up. They're hoping you'll give them a little money in return for a little entertainment. If you have some spare change and if you have had a good time listening or watching, it would be nice to toss in some coins. Don't be intimidated by the dollar bills you may see being offered by others. You can only do what you can do, and whatever it is will surely be appreciated. But remember this: If you can't offer any money, don't feel obligated to keep walking instead of enjoying the sights and sounds. Those people who entertain on the streets don't do it just for money. They also do it because they like feeling appreciated and admired. So pause and enjoy. It won't make them rich, but it will flatter them!

Everybody needs money. Everybody wants money. But not everyone wants or needs the same amount. It depends on how they would like to live and what things are most important to them. How *you* feel about money is a personal thing. If it means a lot, then I hope you get it! If it doesn't, then I hope you have enough to keep you comfortable and safe. But no matter what money means to you, it should not define who you are. Money cannot buy *sensitivity* or *respect*, a sense of *responsibility*, an ability to *compromise*, or *know-how*.

Money cannot buy *social savvy*. Many people think it can, though. They think having money makes anything they do okay. But I know differently. And now, so do you.

NINE

social savvy for delicate times

*T*here are a number of issues in life that are particularly demanding. They require that you do a great deal of independent thinking without being swayed by others, that you face feelings and circumstances you would love to avoid, and that you allow yourself to grow. None of this is easy. Dealing with many of these issues, such as drugs, divorce, prejudice, religion, illness, and your body (its privacy, health, and integrity), is a hard job. But life being the way it is, I can just about assure you that circumstances involving these issues will arise. When they do, you will be unable to look the other way. So you might as well discover how to bring some social savvy to even these most sensitive times.

Before I go any further, however, I do want to say one thing: No one is perfect. Don't even try to be. It isn't going to happen. But you *can* try to square your shoulders, think clearly, and do the best *you* can. Remind yourself that you do have social savvy. Think about being *sensitive, respectful, compromising,* and *responsible* when you must face some of these issues. Take advantage of your considerable *know-how*—and then use your best judgment. Chances are you'll do fine.

drugs

Unfortunately, at some time or other you will probably be confronted with a choice: drugs or no drugs. Friends may suggest you try them. Acquaintances may dangle them before you. Even people you may not know at all might offer you a drug experience. What are you going to do?

Let me begin by saying that I can, to some extent, understand the temptation to try drugs. It is often presented to people your age as a kind of test. If you take drugs, "you're one of us"; if you don't, "you're nobody." Sometimes the decision can seem to be more about keeping friends than about taking drugs. I *do* understand that. But what you need to understand is that the decision you have to make is not about drugs or friends. It just feels that way. What it's really about is *your life*. It's about *your body* and *your mind*. Are you going to keep them healthy or not?

Life isn't a breeze for anyone. Taking drugs can't change the facts. They won't win you true friends or love. They may make you so high that for a while you won't care about your problems—but you will also lose your hold on those things that bring you pleasure. In other words, they will alter how you view everything. When you think about that, it's terrifying.

Perhaps the toughest part of turning down drugs is the pressure you may feel from your crowd—especially if you are feeling low and would like some relief. But there are a few things you should know about this kind of pressure that TV and radio anti-drug campaigns don't explain. And they come under the category, of course, of *social savvy*.

• Kids who insist that you take drugs along with them are looking for approval, not friends. How can they be looking for friends? Drugs make you turn inward and concentrate on your own distorted senses. You can't be a friend to anyone when that is happening. You can't even be a friend to yourself! When kids want you to take drugs, they are really asking you to tell them it's a good thing to do.
• When kids tell you drugs feel great, they forget to mention the price you have to pay for that high. And I don't mean money. The price you pay is that you lose the best protection you have against life's wicked surprises: *You!* When you're on drugs, you are not thinking clearly, or like yourself. The results? You could lose friends, have an accident, get into a fight, cause someone else to get hurt, get into trouble with the law, make the wrong decision in an emergency, or lose the respect of those you most care about. That's quite a price.

• Kids who take drugs do not feel good about themselves. In fact, they feel pretty awful. Otherwise they'd be content to move around their world fully aware of what's going on, tolerating the bad and enjoying the good. And the simple truth about people who don't like themselves is, there's very little room for them to really like someone else. Including you. When a "friend" smiles at you when you agree to take drugs, he or she is not liking you more. He or she is simply feeling a little less alone—at your expense.

So, to sum up, why be pressured into drugs by kids who aren't looking for real friends, don't like themselves anyway, and are setting themselves up for big trouble? Of course, advising you to "just say no" doesn't help much either. Instead, if these people are your friends, you will want to explain yourself in a way that isn't preachy, but rather gentle and matter-of-fact. In so doing, you might even influence a few people to think twice about the drugs they are taking. *That* would be terrific. So here's a brief guide to help you stand your ground with *sensitivity*, *responsibility*, *respectfulness*, and *know-how*. (When it comes to drugs, there's no room for *compromise!*)

A couple of friends try to pressure you into taking drugs, then accuse you of being chicken or immature when you say no.

Don't be defensive. That will keep your friends "on the attack." Remember, they want approval. By saying no, you are in a way threatening them, and they don't like the feeling. Instead, be positive and absolute. "I'm saying no because I feel fine the way I am," followed by a "Why don't we go to the movies or go get some pizza," would be just fine. You are telling your friends how *you* feel and making it clear that you are not rejecting them. If they continue to criticize or push, you may have to look for other friends. Chances are if you hung out with this group too often, you might get into trouble simply by being with them. Drugs are illegal. Don't forget that. If your friends are caught, you'll look guilty too.

You suspect an unhappy girlfriend has secretly started taking drugs.

Tread very gently. if she hasn't told you she's taking drugs, it's probably because she feels embarrassed, scared, or very defensive about her decision. Mostly she might be frightened she'd lose your friendship. If you notice her schoolwork is slipping or that she seems very far away when you talk with her, then say so. Ask her gently if anything is wrong or if you can help her in any way. If she insists everything is fine, let it go for a while. Maybe it is. Maybe she's just blue and doesn't want to discuss her problems. But if the signs that drugs are involved keep multiplying, wait for a quiet moment and then ask. If she says no, then all you can do is keep an eye on her and tell her you'll be there when she wants to talk. But if she says yes, *don't lecture!* First, try to understand her reasons. People often start taking drugs because they feel a lot of intense loneliness. Simply by listening to her you might ease her pain. You will also be helping her to see you're her friend—that you are not sitting in judgment of her. Once you've done that, you might tell her what scares *you* about drugs and then suggest she see a school counselor to help her to stop and to deal with the feelings that made her begin in the first place. Finally, you might assure her that she can talk with you anytime.

You're at a party with some older kids and they ask you to leave early and go get some pizza. As you approach the car, you can see that the driver is drunk.

Don't get in. No ifs, ands, or buts about it. It doesn't matter that you're afraid the others might laugh at you. It doesn't matter that you've already said good-bye to people still at the party. It doesn't matter that they're all going just a few blocks away to the pizza shop. Don't get in. We're not talking about your ego or your hunger pangs. We're talking about *your life*. You have two choices. One would protect only you—which is a start. You could simply stop and say, "You know, I just remembered something I have to do. Go ahead without me." Your other choice is the tougher one, but it might help protect everyone. You could look the driver in the eye and say, "I think you've had a lot to drink and I don't want to go if you're at the wheel." If he starts to laugh at you, you might add something like, "I saw a news program about some people who got really hurt in an accident with a drunk driver. I will never forget it." That statement will at least for a moment stop people cold. It's the kind of remark that makes people think. A few may even get out of the car—including the driver. In that case, a sober person can take the wheel and the pizza trip can proceed!

divorce

Divorce is very painful for everyone, as it changes family life in very significant ways. It's painful for the husband and the wife because they are saying good-bye to an important relationship and because each of them may see a little less of their children. It's painful for the children because they will no longer be living under the same roof at the same time with both parents. Even if there is a great deal of unpleasantness in the house, everyone staying together can sometimes seem better than weathering such a drastic change at home.

If your parents are getting a divorce, it can feel embarrassing, hurtful, horribly sad, and scary. If your friend's parents are getting a divorce, it can feel that way to *both of you*. You might think, "Uh-oh. If they can get divorced, so can my parents." But divorce is not a disease. You can't "catch it." And it's not a crime or a failure. It's a difficult and sad decision made by two people who feel that each of them would be happier apart. And while you may find this hard to understand, it might also mean that in the long run, the children will be happier as well. Growing up in a home where parents are not happy together can often create a very difficult atmosphere. That can cause a lot of problems for everyone. So, what do you do if you find yourself having to deal with divorce in either your family or someone else's?

Your friend tells you her parents are getting a divorce and starts to cry.

Don't tell her lots of people get divorced. That doesn't matter to her. This is her family. Instead, say something like "That's very sad news," and then let her talk about how she feels. Of course, as the conversation goes on, you can suggest that maybe things will be a little less tense at home, or remind her of someone you both know whose parents are divorced but who sees them all the time anyway. The idea is to first be sympathetic. Don't be afraid to deal with your friend's painful feelings. Realize she has to deal with those first before she can move on to happier thoughts.

class quote

"My friend's parents are getting a divorce," a person in my group confessed, "and when she talks about it, she starts to cry. That makes me want to either cry or run." I nodded sympathetically. "It's hard sticking by a friend who is hurting. It's scary too. But if you have to choose between crying and running, I'd suggest you cry . . . and then listen. That will prove you care about her. Running will prove you care about yourself."

Your father has just moved out. Your parents are getting a divorce, but none of your friends know. They just keep asking you where he is.

First of all, you have to remember that a divorce is nothing to be embarrassed about. It is something that happens when two people feel they cannot be happy together any longer. It doesn't even mean that they have failed at marriage, though I confess lots of people may feel that way about themselves. It just means they have grown very much apart and that they do not feel they can be close again. What is embarrassing about that? Your parents' decision to separate has nothing to do with you and has nothing to do with their being "good" or "bad" people. It has to do with life and how things can change in ways we don't expect. The worst thing you can do to yourself during this difficult time is to hide the fact of the divorce. Somehow, hiding things can make them seem *so* much worse than they really are. The very act of hiding can make a person feel guilty and bad. Don't do it! Be honest and straightforward instead. "My parents are getting a divorce." That's all you have to say. If your friends say, "But why?" you don't have to answer. You probably don't even know the answer! A simple "I guess they have their reasons" is good enough. And then, if you want, talk about your feelings. Bottling up difficult emotions can make you feel awful. Letting the hurt out really eases the pain.

Your parents are divorced, and now your mother is being picked up by a date. You're angry and don't want to see him.

It is natural to be angry at your parents for getting a divorce. You want your family all together and they didn't let that happen. But your parents did what they had to do and one thing everyone has a right to do is to get on with their lives. Including you. Your life includes a divorce in the family. It also includes a life with two parents who will want to have dates and perhaps marry again. They want to be happy. No one, I am sure, will be asking you to think of this date as your father or mother. But they will expect that you will treat this person with *respect*. After all, this man is not responsible for your parents' divorce! So try to keep an open mind. Talk with him. Introduce him to your pet or show him your science project. If he asks you about school, answer him nicely. You might just discover he's quite an interesting person. Besides, he's here to try to show your mother a wonderful time. Certainly that ought to be worth a kind word!

prejudice

Prejudice is everywhere. Anytime anyone forms an opinion about someone because of their skin color, religion, finances, address, education, language, age, or country of origin, there is prejudice involved. Why? Because the opinion is formed not only from notions that have nothing to do with the particular person, but also from tired and often dangerous ideas that have been passed down from generation to generation. Something wicked could be said about any group. All rich people are thoughtless. All poor people are dumb. All white people are white-collar criminals. All black people are dangerous. All fat people are messy. All skinny people are nervous. All old people are confused. All young people are irresponsible. All Italians belong to the Mafia. All Russians are spies. Do you see what I mean? Many people even believe that, depending on your religion, you're only interested in money or you're probably very uptight or you're just plain weird. How ridiculous. I know people who love money, are extremely uptight, and are very weird in every religion! Truthfully, if you have any prejudices, you are not entirely to blame. As a very important song in the musical *South Pacific* goes, "You have to be taught to hate and fear. . . ." What does that mean? It means that believing that a certain race or religion or wallet size ought to be shunned or worshiped, has very little to do with personal experience. It's something we are taught. We are not born prejudiced. We become that way when we listen to others. But a truly socially savvy person keeps an open mind. Prejudices die hard. It's very difficult to put aside what you've always thought was true. But it is your *responsibility* to try.

So the next time you feel yourself jumping to conclusions about someone because of what they look like, their heritage, the size of their wallet, or anything else—look again. Listen. Be open. I promise that you are in for a big surprise. And if that skinny person does end up being nervous or that rich person is thoughtless, does it mean that what you've heard all along is true? I say absolutely not. It only means that nervous and thoughtless people come in all kinds of packages— and you happened to have found two of them!

Unfortunately, combating prejudice is not always an easy thing. Situations will come up in which you will feel uncomfortable and moments will arise in which you will actually need to take a stand. Consider the following hypothetical situations for an idea of how a little social savvy can help:

There's a quiet Japanese student on your decoration committee for the dance. She doesn't speak English very well and so everyone is ignoring her, as if she didn't have an opinion.

Frankly, I have never viewed school only as a place to learn reading, writing, and arithmetic. It's also a place to learn about yourself, others, and the world around you. So do it. It's ridiculous to conclude that a person who doesn't speak English well has no feelings, ideas, or interests. This student is a person! It's more work for you, of course, but don't participate in her unhappy acceptance of her lot on this committee. Hold up a color chart and ask her which colors she likes best. Point out the balloons, show her a picture of a refreshment table, and point to some posters, then ask her what she would like to work with the most. Give her a chance! She might have fabulous artistic ability ! You'll never know until you stop assuming she can't help.

There are a few black students in your class who pretty much stick together. You're planning a party for your friends that does not by any means include the whole class—but you do feel bad that you aren't inviting any black kids.

If you are really only inviting the people you are close to, then you have no reason to feel bad. However, you do have reason to stop and think. Are you not friendly with the black kids because they're black or because it is an absolute fact that you have nothing in common with any of them? Perhaps you need to examine the possibility that you are missing out on some good friendships because you keep moving toward only the people who look like you. Putting the party aside, why not make an effort to really get to know a person in your class whose skin color is different from yours? If these more intimate conversations go well, plan to meet for lunch in the cafeteria. Start slowly, as you would with any new friend. The point is, you shouldn't extend invitations out of guilt. They should be given in friendship. Just don't miss out on making those friendships because of surface differences between you.

You're at a party with some friends and one of them tells a racist joke. Everyone around you laughs nervously.

It's not easy to take a stand. And in this case, if no one is directly being hurt by the joke, you may not have to. The only thing you must do is be true to yourself. If you don't think the joke is funny, you can simply not laugh, and if you're really offended, walk away for a moment. You might also choose to say, "That's not so funny," depending on your mood. *However,* if someone standing nearby could be hurt by the joke (if it's a joke about Polish people and a person with a Polish heritage is right there), you might want to be a bit more aggressive. Keeping in mind that sudden bursts of anger don't work very well, you might just say, "I really think you should cut it out. Those kinds of jokes are ugly and unfair." Now, I'm not saying everyone will suddenly see the error of their ways and apologize, or that these friends of yours will want to smother you with hugs. But, you will stop them cold. And, more importantly, you will have protected not only the person who was hurt, but also your own sense of self. It's not fun to follow a crowd when it doesn't feel good. On the other hand, it feels very powerful to know your own mind and to follow your own heart.

religion

Religion is a very important part of many people's lives. How, who, and where each person worships is a personal thing that ought to be *respected* by everyone. Of course, as history has proven, and as we just discussed in the section on prejudice, respecting the religious differences between all of us has not been one of mankind's success stories.

Still, it can be one of yours. In fact, if you ever expect to lay claim to social savvy, it has to be.

But there's another aspect of this as well. And that is *respecting* your own religion and the circumstances in which you worship. Religion is a personal thing, but people often worship in a group. Whether you're at a church or a synagogue, you do have to appreciate the significance of the proceedings for those people who surround you. Of course, this can be especially sticky when you are visiting a friend who is of a different religious persuasion from you, and thus you find yourself at a service you don't understand.

Lots of young people get a bit nervous during religious occasions because the adults around them are usually quite serious. Here's a guide to some common confusions and difficult moments.

You've forgotten the words to a prayer.

Speaking very softly, so as not to disturb those sitting next to you, try to keep up. If you can hardly remember a single word, then stand or sit quietly, and if you feel dreadfully embarrassed, then simply move your lips a little to your own prayer. It's not a crime to forget a prayer. And it is very *respectful* to keep your lapse of memory to yourself.

You've said Merry Christmas to someone who is Jewish.

You may in the spirit of the season sing out a "Merry Christmas!" to a new friend who you just assumed celebrated that holiday. If he or she replies, "Well, actually I'm Jewish and we celebrate Chanukah," don't get upset. It's true one shouldn't assume something about another person just because it's true for you. But again, it's hardly a crime. Nor is it insensitive or cruel. Simply reply something like, "Oh! I didn't know! Happy Chanukah!" And then, if you'd like, you might add, "I'll let you see my Christmas tree if you'll let me see your menorah!" Nothing is nicer than two friends who want to grow to understand each other's important differences—which brings me to the next situation.

Your Catholic friend would like you to attend a Christmas service with her because she thinks you'd enjoy the music. You're scared to go because you're afraid it would feel strange.

It may feel strange. It will certainly be different. But being afraid doesn't make sense. You are who you are. She is not asking you to change that. But she is asking you to appreciate something new. She would like you to see the way in which she and her family worship. That is all. When it comes to social savvy, the truth is, the more you understand the important differences between people, the easier and more confident you will be.

Practically speaking, however, just because you visit a church, you do not have to worship the way the members of that church are worshiping. If your friend visited your service, you would not expect her to know your prayers. All that is expected of you in a place of worship is that you *respect* those people around you and allow them to do as they do.

A friend tells you a religious belief that you find a little offensive. It goes against everything you've ever been taught.

Don't get angry. Unless this friend is trying to convince you to think the same way, what he believes is his business. If you disagree, you can tell him why, but that's all. As long as neither one of you is hurting anyone, you are both entitled to your views. Besides, there are usually no winners when it comes to arguing religious beliefs—just broken friendships.

illness

Illness is upsetting. Sometimes it can be downright scary—especially when it causes pain or threatens the life of someone we know.

We are all afraid of pain and loss, and illness may sometimes carry with it both of these experiences. But like it or not, illness is a part of life and is therefore something you need to face. Shying away from a sick person will probably make both of you feel worse. It can make the person who is ill feel as if nothing else about him or her counts anymore—as if everyone has forgotten he or she could be funny, warm, or interesting. And it can make you feel even more fearful—largely because what you don't know or face is almost always more terrifying than the reality. After all, with proper medical care, lots of people who are quite sick continue to lead very productive lives!

If you know someone who is ill, try not to be afraid of what that means. If they are weak or have to have periodic stays in the hospital or are always having to take medicine, remember that being sick is only one part of who this person really is. He or she still has his or her smarts, humor, drive, and kindness—though it may sometimes be harder to see these qualities. People who are ill can become quite distressed and appear to lose the positive side of their personalities. Understand that and try to stick with it. You are bound to cheer up your friend and in so doing keep a very important friendship—for both of you—thriving.

Your friend was in a terrible accident and has to be in the hospital for over a month. She wants you to come as often as possible, but hospitals make you feel sick. You keep trying to come up with excuses.

Hospitals make a lot of people feel terrible. The sights, sounds, and smells all come together to remind us that being sick can be very unpleasant and even lonesome. It's little wonder visiting a hospital feels bad. The problem is, your sick friend deserves more attention than your fears. Going to the hospital to keep her company is an important, though difficult, part of being her friend. If you cannot go every other day to the hospital, as your friend has requested, fine. If there's a phone in her room, call every day! Walking in as white as a sheet and feeling faint is not going to help your friend very much, anyhow! But you will have to screw together your courage and go every few days. If necessary, keep your mind focused on something light. As you walk down the halls, keep your eyes straight ahead and recite the names of as many states as you can remember. If you hear something unpleasant, pretend you are an actress in a movie or soap opera. Murmur a hokey script line to yourself. It will make you smile, and *that* will make you feel better. And whatever you do, once you're in the room with your friend, concentrate on *her*. Even if she wants to hear about *you* and what's going on in your life, tell her, but edit yourself. Leave out how you feel about hospitals. She'll only feel even worse. When the visit is over, do something nice for yourself. Take a walk in the sun. Treat yourself to a milk shake. Remind yourself of how pleasant your life really is. And feel VERY VERY lucky.

A friend's father is dying. He's so upset, you often feel like you are with a stranger. Sometimes you notice he's been crying. He is rarely funny anymore, and he loses his temper a lot. Still, he hardly talks about his father at all.

Unfortunately, people learn at a very young age that pleasant news is easy to share with friends. Painful news is not. The truth is, most people would rather listen to good news. Bad or sad news is hard to hear. Your friend might be feeling that the tragic news in his life is just too painful to share—that you wouldn't want to listen and that it's just too horrible for him to even discuss. This is natural. But it is to a large extent why he is behaving in such a difficult fashion. There is *so* much locked up inside.

A good friend in this situation would try to gently and *sensitively* draw him out. You shouldn't push. It's possible your friend doesn't want to get too close to his raw painful feelings. But, on the other hand, he may want to talk and is afraid to do so. If you'd like, bring the subject up yourself. Tell him you're so sorry about his father and ask how he is feeling. Don't be afraid to bring it up. If he can see you are willing to talk, he may find the courage to open up. You may even see a glimpse of his old humor and warmth. It's still there, you know. It's just being overwhelmed by a very powerful and painful life experience.

Someone you know well has passed away and you would like to say something to the family. The problem is, you don't know what to put in the note.

Sympathy notes are always difficult to write. But when you think about it, they really shouldn't be so hard at all! After all, in them you can express not only your sadness, but also your good feelings. In fact, sympathy notes are essentially complimentary. Consider these possibilities.

> *Dear Mrs. Smith,*
> *I was so sorry to hear of your husband's death. He always had a smile and a joke for me when I came into his store and I will miss him a lot. My thoughts are with you.*
>
> > *Sincerely,*
> > *Jim*

> *Dear Lisa,*
> *I heard about your grandmother's death just this morning. I know how much you loved her and I wanted you to know I'm thinking of you. If there's anything I can do to help you, please call.*
>
> > *Love,*
> > *Helen*

As you can see, sympathy notes say nice things about the people who have died, allow the survivors to know they are not alone in their grief, and can express your desire to help. These thoughts are very nice! So don't avoid them *or* the note writing. People who are in mourning appreciate the kind messages very much.

your body

Your body belongs to you. Only you can really protect its privacy, health, and integrity. What do I mean by integrity? Your body's private space. I mean your right to do with your body as you see fit: If you feel someone is standing too close, step away. If someone is touching you even in the most innocent way and it bothers you, say no and take a step away. I cannot state this strongly enough.

At the beginning of this chapter I spoke of the five qualities that comprise social savvy. They are *sensitivity, respect, responsibility, compromise, and know-how.* As with drugs, when it comes to your body, *compromise* does not apply. What you do with your body or what you allow to happen to it must be a decision you make based solely on how *you* feel.

Yes, you should be sensitive toward others. If you don't want someone to put their arm around you, it isn't necessary to yell, "Stop it!" You can simply gently pull away. In this way you are being *responsible* and *respectful* to yourself, and you are taking care of the situation with a good deal of savvy *know-how.* But you are *not,* nor should you be, compromising. And this goes for friends, relatives, or acquaintances.

The problem is, sometimes protecting your privacy and integrity can be a bit tricky—not to mention embarrassing. Your body is changing a lot these days. Yours may be maturing slowly or quickly. Either way, it can bring up confused feelings that may lead you to feel especially private about yourself. Here is a list of common situations young people find themselves in and a few hints on how to get through them as smoothly as possible.

You're in a store with a friend looking for new clothes and she wants to come into the dressing room with you. You are very embarrassed and wish she wouldn't.

Just say, "I'd rather go in by myself. I'll come out and show you if I think it looks good." Your friend may look at you a little hurt or confused, but just smile at her warmly, and do exactly as you say. She'll soon forget about it. After all, there's a lot of clothing to look at outside that dressing room!

An older boy is talking to you outside of school and all of a sudden he puts his arm around you in a very personal way. He's very cute, but you feel a little overwhelmed.

First and foremost, pay attention to your instincts. If it doesn't feel right, then chances are it isn't right for you. Still, you don't want to offend him because you find him attractive and it's so much fun to be noticed by an older guy. You can very gently pull away a bit, and pretend to tie your shoe, or rearrange your books or look for a friend. Once that's done, be sure to stand a safe distance from him so that it is not quite so easy for him to be so familiar. Keep up the friendly chat, however. It's an important way to communicate that you like him.

You and the rest of the guys are in the locker room for a shower. Everyone is kind of parading around the space looking at one another's bodies, but you don't want to do that.

Then don't. Keep a towel nearby and as soon as you step out of the shower, wrap it around your waist. If someone challenges you or accuses you of being too modest or ashamed of your body, stand tall. "I'm not interested in looking at your body. I don't know why you're so interested in mine" will quiet them pretty fast. Whatever you do, don't say, "I am not ashamed" or "I am not modest." That would just invite the guys to insist you prove it—which is exactly what you want to avoid.

A friend of your parents touches you in a way that you think isn't right. You're not sure why, but whenever it happens, you have to fight the urge to pull away.

Don't fight the urge. You are probably very tempted to just sit still because you can't believe this person could be doing something wrong. After all, he's a friend of your parents. Well, the truth is, he may not be doing anything wrong. It may just be your particular sensitivity at this time. But you know what? So what? It doesn't matter what the reason is. If you don't feel comfortable, it's wrong for you. And that is all that counts.

Again, gently pull away. If he persists—hugging you too close or tickling you in a way you don't like or stroking your hair—then speak up. "Please don't do that. It makes me feel uncomfortable" would do nicely. Even a "You know, I really don't like being touched that much," said with a nice smile, would be fine. Remember, it's your body. Only you can give it the protection it deserves. You, that is, and your parents. Give them a chance to know what you are feeling. It's important to all of you.

When it comes to drugs, divorce, prejudice, religion, illness, and your body, a little social savvy can go a long way. These are sensitive and often difficult issues, which demand a lot from the people involved. But you can do it. You simply have to think for yourself, do your best to understand others, and *always* leave room for your own personal growth. If you feel that some things are too tough to handle, try a little at a time, anyway. You might be surprised to discover how strong and able you really are!

savvy asides: an epilogue

I hope this book will be a big help to you as you move through your life. Though this book is not a cure for life's problems, it can give you the confidence you need to move through good and bad times feeling strong and sure. Whether you're eight years old or eighty years old, the information on these pages still applies. Social savvy is a wonderful skill you can use at all times.

Finally, there were a number of savvy moves I never did find the right place for in this book. I think they are as good a way as any to conclude this book.

miss judith's closing thoughts

• When the elevator doors slide open, always step to the side to let people off before you get on. If there is an operator, say thank you.
• When walking up or down stairs, stay to your right.
• If you notice someone has dropped something on the street, pick it up and get their attention by saying, "Excuse me . . ."
• If you think a teacher has said something incorrect, don't shout out, "Mrs. Lucas! You made a mistake!" That's too challenging, disrespectful, and embarrassing. Raise your hand and when you're called, say, "When you said that . . . I was confused. I always thought that . . ." Teachers have feelings too.
• If you are seated on a crowded bus and an old person gets on, give him or her your seat—unless you are ill.

• If you don't like someone, keep it to yourself. No need to list a person's bad qualities, as you see them, to someone else.

• Never shout across the room at a restaurant, party, movie, or any other public place. If you see someone you know, walk over.

• If you are sitting in the backseat of a car and the person in the middle is being dropped off first, don't expect him or her to climb over you. Get out, let him or her get out, and then move back inside.

• If someone brings up a subject you know nothing about, don't pretend you do just to stay in the conversation. You will likely give yourself away. If you want to participate, ask questions. There is no reason to think you have to know something about everything. It's savvy to learn. It's silly to pretend you already know.

• When you go through a door, hold it for the next person. If someone holds it for you, say thank you.

• If you open a box of candy or cookies in front of friends, offer a piece to everyone. If you don't want to share, then don't open a thing until you're alone.

• If your basketball team loses, remember to congratulate the winners. They deserve it, and you would have appreciated the gesture if you had won. Besides, doing so underlines the most important part of competition—to do your best and enjoy the challenge, no matter who comes out on top.

In fact, that's a good way to approach life.

index

acceptance, in friendships, 50, 52
accidents:
    at friend's house, 144, 150
    in restaurants, 95, 99, 115
accusing, helping vs., 58, 185
adults, 136, 200
    conversation with, 39
    introduction of, 36, 37
    unwelcome attention from, 198–99
    see also parents
affection, conversation and, 27
alcohol, at parties, 130, 185–86
allergies, 146, 153
allowances:
    negotiation of, 164–65
    unfixed, 165–66
anger:
    in conversations, 43–44
    friendships threatened by, 68–69
    problem-solving and, 70, 71–72
apples, eating of, 93–94
arguments, *see* conflicts
arrivals, 85
    of house guests, 147, 153–54
    of party guests, 129
    at restaurants, 104–5
artichokes, eating of, 94–95
asking questions:
    in conversations, 30–34, 37, 201
    dangerous topics in, 33–34
asparagus, eating of, 95
attention, conversation and, 27

bad influences, parents' concern
    about, 65–66
balancing friendships, 61–64

bananas, eating of, 95–96
bar/bas mitzvahs, 139–40
bathroom etiquette, for house guests,
    147, 149–50, 153, 157
beds, house guests and, 151, 152
"best friend," replacing of, 70
body, integrity of, 197–99
body language, 28–30, 47
borrowing:
    friendships and, 55, 56, 57, 172
    money from parents, 166
braces, food caught in, 91
bread and butter, eating of, 91
breaking dates, 62–63
budgets, for parties, 122–23
buffet tables, 81–82
bus boys, 107

cancelling reservations, 104
car etiquette, 201
centerpieces, in table settings, 82–83,
    89, 139
charity work, 178–80
checks, restaurant, 117–19
    how to ask for, 119
    mistakes on, 26, 118
"chemistry," in friendships, 49–50
"chicken," accusations of, 18, 183–84
chicken, fried, eating of, 97
clams and oysters, eating of, 96
clean ups:
    house guests and, 149–50, 152, 156
    for parties, 127, 131–32
coat checks, 104, 120
cocktail napkins, 80, 81
cold-shoulder responses, 69

judgmental attitude, friendships and, 58

kissing, introductions and, 36
kitchen etiquette, for house guests, 148, 156
knife and fork, how to use, 92–93
know-how, 16, 24–26, 200
    questionnaire on, 24–25

leaving food on plate, 88
lemon, inadvertent squirting of, 99
letters and notes:
    apology, 144
    invitations, 125
    sympathy, 196–97
    thank-you, 136–37, 151–52
    written but not sent, 71
lingering:
    at parties, 131, 136
    in restaurants, 119
liquor, at parties, 130, 185–86
listening, in conversations, 30, 34, 35, 43–44, 185
listing of friends' good qualities, 71
loans, from family, 166
lobster, eating of, 97–98
loyalty, in friendships, 51, 59, 61

maître d's, 104–5, 111, 119–20
mediating, in friendships, 63–64
menus, 106–7, 138–39, 153, 158
    foreign words on, 108–10
    for parties, 123, 126–27, 130
mistakes, learning from, 17, 18
money issues, 13, 167–81
    family attitudes and, 163–68
    friends and, 168–72
    jobs and, 173–78
    sensitivity rules for, 170–72
    worth measured by, 167, 181
mourning, 195–96

names:
    forgetting of, 36
    in introductions, 35–37
napkins:
    etiquette for, 86, 89
    in table settings, 78, 80, 82, 83
nervousness, conversation and, 27

noise levels, at parties, 131, 135
noncompetitiveness, in friendships, 50, 53–54
nonsmoking areas, in restaurants, 106

older people, courtesy to, 200
olive pits, 92
openers, in conversation, 37–38, 137
ordering in restaurants, 107–10, 116

packing, for house visit, 145–47
paper plates, 84
parents:
    divorce and, 186–88
    of friends, 66–67, 139, 151–52, 153
    friendships and, 64–67
    house rules and, 142, 145, 154, 158
    money issues and, 163–68
    party rules and, 129, 131–32
    rudeness to, 64–65
parties, 12–13, 121–41
    checklist for, 129–32
    guests at, 13, 121, 123–24, 130, 132–41
    host/hostess of, 121, 122, 129–32
    planning of, 121–29
    special, 137–41
    taking charge at, 130, 131, 135
party books, 132
patience, in friendships, 50, 52–53
pears, eating of, 93–94
peas, eating of, 98
perfection, attitude toward, 182
pets, 146
picking up, helpful, 200
picnics, utensils for, 84–85
place cards, 84, 138
place mats, in table settings, 80, 81
plastic dinner dishes, 83–84
plastic utensils, 78, 84
popularity, 59–61
    power and, 60
power fingers, 92, 93
prejudice, combating of, 188–91
pretensions, ignorance and, 201
privacy:
    in money matters, 163, 169, 170–72
    of own body, 197–99
    in restaurants, 115, 117

index

ABOUT THE AUTHOR

Judith Ré is the founder and president of the Judith Ré Academie for Instruction in the Social Graces. She is a recognized expert on etiquette, and directs programs for children and adults in various cities across the nation. She has been the subject of numerous print and broadcast interviews, both in the United States and abroad. Judith lives in Boston with her husband and daughter.

ABOUT THE WRITER

Meg Schneider is a New York-based book packager and writer. She is the author of numerous self-help books for teenagers, which focus on emotional and practical issues, and is currently at work on her second novel for young readers. She holds a Master's in Counseling Psychology.